new dress a day

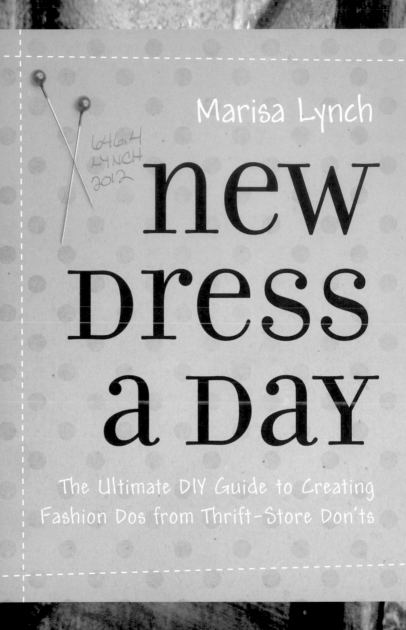

Marisa Lynch

646.4
LYNCH
2012

new dress a day

The Ultimate DIY Guide to Creating Fashion Dos from Thrift-Store Don'ts

BALLANTINE BOOKS　NEW YORK

A Ballantine Books Trade Paperback Original

Copyright © 2012 by Marisa Lynch
Photographs copyright © 2012 by Jordan Whitley

Published in the United States by Ballantine Books, an imprint of
The Random House Publishing Group, a division of Random House, Inc., New York.

BALLANTINE and colophon are registered trademarks of Random House, Inc.

Portions of this work originally appeared on the author's blog, New Dress a Day
(www.newdressaday.com).

ISBN 978-0-345-53288-6
eBook ISBN 978-0-345-53289-3

Printed in China

www.ballantinebooks.com

9 8 7 6 5 4 3 2 1

To the crafty lads and lasses in all of us.
It's there, I promise.

My heart completely dropped the moment my co-worker walked out of the conference room and slid her finger across her neck. I was summoned next, rubbing my sweaty palms against my skirt as I slowly walked in. My boss and his minion did their work quickly, letting me know that by June 1st, I would no longer be employed at the small Los Angeles–based online magazine where I'd been working for the past two years. It felt like time stopped and I was frozen in my steps. I was having my Jerry Maguire moment, except I didn't write a mission statement and there was no Renée Zellweger choosing to come along on the ride of joblessness with me. I was breathless, caught off guard, and completely unsure of the next step—where do I even begin?

My thirtieth birthday was right around the corner, and I was in a major funk—completely at a loss as to what my next step would be, surprisingly helpless and confused. I mean, I was a grown woman and I had no plan! I'd always thought that by thirty I would have my sh*t together—I didn't care about getting married or having kids quite yet, but I didn't think I would be stressing about money or bills, or how to pay bills without money!

I signed up for unemployment and began the job search—to no immediate avail. I was bummed out, trapped in a rut, and needed some sort of outlet, aside from rereading Judy Blume's *Are You There God, It's Me, Margaret* and subbing in Marisa instead of Margaret. Since my gym membership was now canceled and I no longer had a cardio-kickbox-yoga-robics class for relieving stress, I wandered into a movie theater one afternoon to escape my tortuous thoughts and repetitive worries. I went to see *Julie & Julia,* and that's when everything changed.

I left the theater feeling three ways:

1. Obsessed—Clearly, I loved Meryl Streep and how seamlessly she pulled off Julia Child. I loved the clothes Julia wore, the way she threw herself into her cooking, and the way her personality always shined through—completely charming and lovely.
2. Starving—Watching food on a BIG screen for two hours will make anyone hungry, no matter how much popcorn and Junior Mints are consumed during the run time. (It was like I was hungrier after the movie, even though I was snacking throughout. How is that even possible?)
3. Jealous—I desperately wanted what Julie Powell had. Amy Adams (who played her) tapped into what made Julie happy and what gave her daily joy and a respite from an uninspiring job. That is what I wanted and, ultimately, what I needed.

The movie lit a fire under me. I couldn't cook a coq au vin to save my life, but I knew there was one thing I could do really, really well: sew.

The DIY bug bit me early in life. I'd always loved clothes and was obsessed with Elsa Klensch and her show, *Style with Elsa Klensch,* on CNN in my teens. When everyone else was wearing J.Crew and Gap, I hit up local thrift stores and had a blast scouring the aisles for designer garb on the cheap that I could embellish and make my own. My mom was a home economics major, back when you could still major in home ec., and between watching her and crafting patchwork pillows and teal-colored sweatshirts (hey, it was the '90s!) in my middle school Home & Careers classes, I picked up the basics. I learned to sew on a gigantic, thirty-pound sewing machine, perfecting one-of-a-kind purses and creating my own outfits like the TV Kellys I was obsessed with back then: Kelly Taylor (*90210*) and Kelly Kapowski (*Saved by the Bell*). You can see how much quality TV I watched as a teen.

Right after college I made my first big purchase—a sewing machine of my own. My first full-time job was a low-rung entertainment industry gig (the lovely world of casting), and I was netting enough to cover my rent, bills, and gas, but really didn't have any extra cash to spend on clothes. Seeing actors come in each day looking fabulous for their auditions, I started trying to make my own versions of their super-chic, Barneys-purchased ensembles for a fraction of the price.

I spent weekends hanging out at flea markets and checking the paper and Craigslist for the best (and closest) garage sales. In my shopping journeys I would always find awesome pieces but they were either too big, awkwardly ripped, or badly stained. This deterred me at first, but then I began thinking of how, with just a few tweaks, I could have pieces that fit like a glove. Inspiration took over and I began making stuff on my own . . . stuff that cost about half the price of my caffeinated beverages at Starbucks. Kate Bosworth once made my day, complimenting me on my shoes: a pair of pointy-toed flats I snagged at Marshalls on the cheap, with a vintage earring clasped to the top.

So fast-forward again to the summer of 2009—laid off, in the final stages of being twenty-nine, and freaking the F out, I emerged from *Julie & Julia* with an idea: For one year, make one new outfit every day, spending only one dollar per outfit. I'd blog about the results, and call it "New Dress a Day."

I decided I would forgo trips to Bloomies and Nordstrom, say goodbye to H&M and impulsive accessory grabbing at Forever 21! Instead, the only shopping I'd do for a year would be for previously worn pieces that I would fix up myself. I got out my trusty sewing machine, ready to change hems, cut sleeves, and tweak. My goal was to transform a low-budget piece that had its moment back in 1976 and give it another shot today, updated and refreshed. One person's trash became this guerrilla seamstress's treasure. I'd blog and post pictures about my DIY creations: 365 days, 365 items of clothing, 365 dollars. Holy snap, I had found my calling!

I can pretty much guarantee that if you ask anyone about putting together an outfit for a buck, there would be heckling, hoots, and hollers coming from all corners of the blogosphere. However, I documented my transformations meticulously, with photos and steps galore, and I proved it could be done. If you build it, they will come . . . or in my case, if you can buy it on the cheap and sew it on the easy, they will come . . .

I started by documenting the creation of my thirtieth-birthday dress—my first post. After about two months in and sixty dresses down the line, other people, people who I didn't know or share the same bloodline with, started responding, big-time. First, I sent the link to my friends about a week in—I wanted to make sure my compadres saw that I was serious about my project—and they sent it to their friends, who sent it to their friends, and so on, and my traffic started to grow. In the beginning, my blog was featured on green sites like Treehugger.com and craft sites like craftgossip.com, then editorial requests began coming in for actual magazine features. The momentum kept building until the big day: August 17, 2010, approximately 10:37 P.M. PST (if you wanted the specifics). That was the day Yahoo! featured me on its home page, the day my blog received 1,000,000 hits! It was also the day that my BlackBerry ultimately short-circuited (just like Number 5—homage to one of my fave robot movies). Requests came pouring in from national television talk shows and news sites—the media frenzy was on!

Who knew that the little blog I started to help lift me out of my creative funk and make me feel good about all the not-so-good stuff going on in my life would bring all this goodness my way? Who knew that so soon after losing my job, I'd be sharing the stage with Nate Berkus, getting my makeup done before going live on CBS with Erica Hill, and having Giuliana Rancic introduce a segment about me? And that not long after, I'd be putting the finishing touches on my first book! Um, I just pinched myself again.

contents

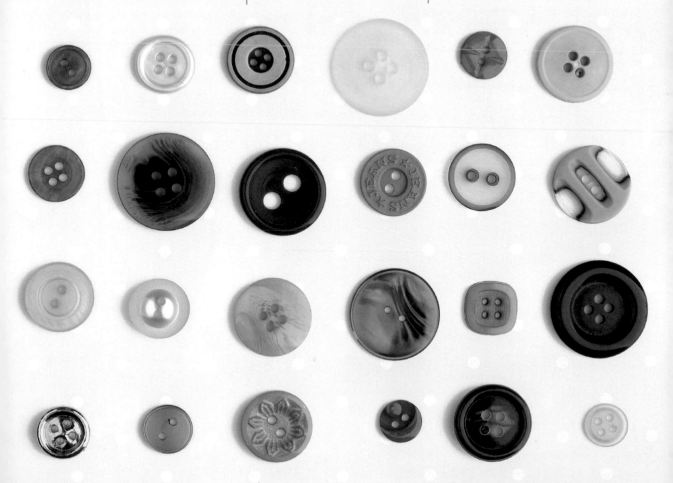

I wanted to write a book that would be a compilation of fun makeovers and crafty tips and a handheld guide to all you need to know to get your sew or no-sew on, not to mention something that can be accessed regardless of whether or not the Internet is working—sorry unnamed Internet provider whose representatives I've spent enough time on the phone with that they can be considered family by now! In these pages, you'll find some of the most talked-about creations from my blog along with a bevy of new projects and stories I've never shared. This is the bring along to craft nights, tote along to thrift stores, have on hand at Jo-Ann Fabric and Craft Stores, book that fits in a recycled tote or very large purse. (One man's airplane carry-on is another man's purse, so what, who cares?!) I'm a highlighter/notemaker/Post-it addict and love having actual books to pull from and reference, so I wanted this to be just that. Somewhere to have all your "dressipes" in one spot as well as places to make notes, keep thread colors, elastic measurements, thrift store recommendations, and the names of awesome associates at Michaels who always help a sistah out.

INTRODUCTION
about this book

Each chapter is defined by a unique theme or style. And for each project, you'll find sew and no-sew options (when available), offering up different routes for you to reach the same end result. We can all be Marthas no matter which path we take toward the finish line.

Does everyone have to own a sewing machine? Pffff, no! Does everyone have to be proficient with a needle and thread? Um, nope! Does everyone have to have an open mind to try and be as creative as possible? Absolutely!

This book isn't about perfection, it's about feeling good and trying your crafty best. You can think of me as that really cool teacher who doesn't give midterms, but instead doles out bright, shiny, sequined stars for participation—and definitely no detention.

To Mrs. Sherman who gave me detention for running in the halls back in middle school, not cool.

I'm a guerrilla seamstress. I didn't go to fashion school or major in fashion design. I'm a rough-and-tumble, come up with something on the fly to figure it out, kind of gal. For my dresses, I'm just using the skills I learned as a teen and pairing them with tricks I've picked up along the way. I'm not perfect, but I make it work, or at least try to.

I encourage you to be creative and not to worry about mistakes—they happen to the best of us. Just know you'll get better the more you practice. Cliché, yes, but totally true.

The first time I tried to drive I was using both feet and had the brake pedal pushed the whole time, thinking that was fine. Since then I've worked my way into Good Driver discount status with my insurance, so that right there is a faux-pas-turned-hur-rah!

Use this book as if it's me sitting right next to you while you use a seam ripper to remove an appliqué, or glue rhinestones to a purse. It's a petite version of me to carry around in your bag while you sift through estate sale treasures. I'm very excited to be hanging with you—if only I could actually enjoy chicken sandies at Chick-fil-A and have happy hour with you too, then that would be complete aces.

the basics

Filling up a grocery cart is a no-brainer: fruits and veggies, Ben & Jerry's half baked Fro Yo, Reduced Fat Cheez-Its, and Dunkin' Donuts ground coffee are my staples. However, what to put in a sewing kit, especially if you're new to the sewing game, can be a bit trickier than choosing what kind of cereal to get.

I remember sifting through my mom's sewing box as a kid and looking at the different colored spools and bobbins as well as some weird looking, razor-ruler thingamajig (sliding gauge), metal claspy thingies (presser-foot replacements), and a plastic red thing (thimble) that looked like it should be a piece on my Monopoly board. The idea of a sewing kit full of these random things may be a little daunting to a newbie. At first they were foreign objects to me too. Only years later do I fully understand their purpose. It has taken some time to procure my dream sewing kit, but if you're impatient (which is usually me on the regular) here's a cheat sheet for the basics to fill your first sewing kit!

the essentials

Bobbins: If you use a sewing machine, you know how important a bobbin is. These plastic or metal miniature wheels wind thread and are inserted underneath the needle plate. Depending on how many projects you've got going on at once, multiple bobbins with multiple thread shades are a treat to have, just so you don't have to rewind each time you sew a different colored fabric. If one disappears after an accidental drop **(those measly little suckers)** you won't be in despair and forced to wait until the fabric store opens to pick up more. ($1+) *(Also see "Bobbins" on p. 9)*

Elastic: It's stretchy, comes in handy when straps break, and is easy to replace when waistlines become too stretched out. Available in a variety of widths—though usually in white (black and assorted colors can be found as well)—elastic should find a spot in your kit. ($0.50+)

Embellishments (buttons, rhinestones, ribbons, trim, and colorful accents): These are all awesome extras to keep in your sewing kit. Sometimes extra matching buttons are found sewn inside a garment. You never know when you'll need a rainbow ribbon to make a belt or some rhinestones to cover up a spot!

Glues: For quick adhesive options, glue rules!
• **Glue guns** are a necessity for adhering ribbon to a clip or feathers to a purse. Easy to use; just plug it in, add a glue stick, and wait for it to warm up. It's a gun that you can't get arrested for using . . . just be careful of the hot metal tip!

Using glue guns often leaves spider-webby strings behind on your fabric. To get rid of these, take a hair dryer, wave it over the strings, and watch them vanish and melt away like the Wicked Witch of the West. Mwahahaha.

• **Aleene's** makes a great assortment of non-hot glues: Fabric Fusion fastens trims and fabrics together. Glitter & Gem Glue affixes those blingy rhinestones. Flexible Stretchable Fabric Glue binds ribbons or other embellishments to stretchy fabrics.
• **Krazy Glue and E-6000** are both ridiculously strong glues perfect for fixing broken buttons or gluing pinbacks to vintage Bakelite charms or felted flowers.
• **Fray Check** is a glue-adjacent liquid. It's not sticky, but when added to the bottom of cut fabric, it stops ragged edges from forming without any sewing. ($1+)

Marking utensils: Chalk, fabric crayons, and Sharpies are just a few of many tools you can use to mark your fabrics. For working on lighter colored fabrics and making marks that shouldn't be apparent, the best devices are neutral (pencil, fabric crayon, or invisible ink marker) or erasable (invisible ink marker or chalk). A Sharpie can do the trick for making lines that won't be seen or marking spots to glue rhinestones—but be careful, this ink is permanent. ($1+)

Needles: Basic hand needles, or "sharps," are about one to two inches long on average, with a round eye (the hole where the thread is pulled through) and a medium-sized point (for sticking through the fabric). It's always good to have a stash of hand-stitching needles nearby. A pack of assorted hand-stitching needles is your best bet—you'll get a mix of all sizes and will have plenty of options to choose from, depending on what you're sewing, as different fabrics warrant different needles.

Sewing-machine needles are sized according to the fabric being sewn. Thinner needles work with thinner/finer fabrics, and thicker needles work with thicker/heavier fabrics—you won't want a thick needle to pierce a fine silk, leaving holes in the fabric, right? The technical scale works like this—the thinner the needle, the lower the number (i.e., American scale 8, 9 or European scale 60, 70) and the thicker the needle, the higher the number (i.e., American scale 18, 19 or European scale 100, 110). Sewing-machine needles also have a sharp edge and an eye on one end, but have a shaft and a shank area (rounded on one side and flat on the other end) that is secured into the sewing machine. For starters, universal or ballpoint needles are standard enough to work well with your cottons and knits. Start off here and you'll have your basics, with regard to needles, covered. ($2+) (Also see "Machine Needles" on p. 9)

Needle threader: Some days the thread just doesn't want to agree with the eye of the needle. A needle threader comes in handy during these times. It's a small gadget with a round tin or plastic head and a diamond-shaped piece of wire attached. You put the wire piece through the eye, then loop the thread through the wire, and pull the wire and thread through the eye, successfully threading the needle. This can be found among the notions in the craft store. ($1+)

Ruler/yardstick: You'll need something to assist in drawing a straight line on your pieces when not cutting freehand. Rulers, yardsticks, or even a phone book will do. (Free+)

Safety pins: For pinchin' and cinchin'. Any size and color of safety pins will do. Get an assortment to keep on hand for mishaps! ($1+)

Scissors: If you can, invest in a good pair because they'll instantly become your BFF. You want a pair about six to eight inches in length that can easily cut through different

TAKING BABY STEPS

The idea of cutting through a garment with a pair of scissors can be very scary; however, the more you cut, the better you'll become! Practice with old dish towels or rags to start, then work your way up to an actual garment. Good thing you can find thrifted pieces on the cheap to test the waters! If you make a few mistakes, no biggie.

kinds of fabrics, so make sure you feel comfortable holding them, and test them out pre-purchase. Steel or nickel-plated scissors are ideal, especially a pair that can be sharpened when it becomes dull. Budget scissors can also do the trick, but need to be replaced more often. I use my mom's Singer pair from her college days and they're amazing. Fiskars, Kai, and Gingher make excellent snippers as well. ($8–$30+)

Seam ripper: This is one of my favorite tools—it makes removing stitches (without ripping the fabric) a breeze. It's basically a plastic stick with a sharp metal point. Another point has a red ball on the end; the end with the ball slides between the seam to cut through the thread. The sharp end is also great for taking out individual stitches, like the ones that keep on embellishments or buttons. This handheld tool ranges in size: I have a mini (two and a half inches) in my to-go kit and a traditional size (five inches) that I use at home. ($2+)

Sewing box: Be it a true sewing box, plastic shoebox, old cigar box **(I had one when I was a kid to hold beads)**, thread organizer, or travel makeup case—whatever works for you—you need something to house your necessities. I've got an assortment of plastic flour and sugar jars, photo boxes, plastic compartmental boxes from Ikea, and an old Clinique travel case as parts of my compound in Sew World, USA. Yeah, I see it as a little neighborhood in a very chic village. (Free+)

Sewing machine: The main event! From boutique sewing stores and mass merchandisers to garage sales and online sites, machines can be found all over the place. Try to test them out first to see what model will suit your sewing needs best, unless you're being given Aunt Patti's old one, in which case you graciously accept regardless! For more advice on machine sewing, check out p. 7. (Used $60+)

Stitch Witchery: A no-sew wonder that fuses two fabrics together. This thinner, feltlike material comes rolled up like a spool of ribbon, and once placed between two fabrics and ironed down, it binds them together. For the non-sewers and sewers looking for a shortcut without consequences, Stitch Witchery is like Glinda the Good Witch in this Emerald City of Sewing. ($3+)

Straight pins and pincushions: Pins are a necessity in the sewing game and they keep hems in place prior to sewing. They also work well as temporary holding devices to test locations for vintage patches or appliqués before actually sewing them down. Straight pins with glass or plastic balls on the head, flat heads, or stainless-steel dressmaker pins are all basic options to pick from. Pins range in size—the larger the millimeters (mm), the thicker the pin.

Make sure you've got a pincushion to house your pins because it's not fun to accidentally step on a rogue one. Anything that will keep the pins together works, from the stuffed tomato or Grabbit Magnetic Pincushion to old, holey, rolled-up socks. **Well, except for your mouth—it's not a proper, safe, or sanitary pincushion—no matter how easy and close by it is!** (Pins $1+, Pincushions Free–$2+)

Tape measure: A handy, flexible ruler of sorts that can measure fabric length as well as your waist and hips! (Lots of fabric stores hand these out as promotional freebies.) (Free+)

Thimble: A traditional steel or nickel-plated thimble or a rubber thimblette are good to have on hand—literally and figuratively. They will help push the needle through thicker fabric so you won't poke and injure your fingers. I have one and rarely use it because I think I'm tough, but I curse my stupidity each time I get pricked. Lots of times they come with travel sewing kits. PS: Don't try to use the one that comes with a Monopoly game. ($1+)

Thread: Black, neutral, and white for sure—other colors can follow. Keep your eyes peeled for 50-wt (this is a pretty universal weight standard) in cotton or polyester (which tends to be cheaper too!). There will be 30-wt and 40-wt's out there as well, but just keep in mind that the higher the number, the finer the thread. ($1+)

Velcro: Fast fabric fasteners (say that three times fast) that offer a quick fix for making things stick. These hook-and-loop pieces with adhesive backings work like this: One side is fuzzy, the other side is prickly, and when they touch, they stick together! Velcro comes in a variety of styles and sizes, from strips you can custom cut to ready-made circles and squares to use in place of metal hook-and-eye closures or zippers. ($1+)

Where to purchase the essentials?

- Craft stores like Michaels and Jo-Ann's—you'll find everything on the list.
- Mass merchandisers like Target and Walmart.
- Drugstores and 99-Cent stores.
- eBay or etsy.com— You can find everything here, just beware of shipping costs.
- Hotels—Many hotels have travel sewing kits (needles, a little bit of thread, and safety pins) in the rooms! Snag some for free next time you're on the road.

safety

If I can offer any words of advice on the safety front, they are: Don't Rush! Slow Down!

Even though Paula Abdul told us to "Rush, Rush," we don't need to hurry when sewing. The last thing you want to do is pierce through anything other than fabric. **(I'm talkin' 'bout fingers, friends.)** Needle through skin is not pleasant, and needle through nail is even more unpleasant—take it from someone who has done just that.

Who's got two thumbs and sewed right through her index finger? This gal! They don't call me Olive Oyl for nothing!

This is true not only with your handheld needle and thread, but especially when using the sewing machine. Take your time. Even if you're supposed to meet friends at 9:00 P.M. to make it to a birthday party before parking spaces get taken and it's now 8:15 P.M., and you still have more work to finish on your fun party dress, don't try to sew at epic speeds to make it in time. Screw the parking spaces and just cab it.

 tend to make up my own vocabulary at times. For example, "boobal," the area on a lady where her bosom resides. Bosom sounds weird coming out of my mouth, whereas boobal just makes sense.

marisaisms/
sewingology

Other words that just make sense to me and may tickle your fancy as well:

Blerg as Tina Fey would say on *30 Rock*. For all the bad words you really want to say. Also crapola, ugly.

Boobal the area on a woman where her bosom resides.

Campees another word for campers.

Chestal same as boobal (above).

DIY Do It Yo'self—just keepin' it real by making it on your own!

Dressipe my recipes for making dresses!

ECU! Extreme Close-Up! (Also the letters of my parents' alma mater.)

Ensemble-y challenged made famous in *Clueless*—those with problems putting together outfits.

Fance short for fancy. Something that is perfect for dressier occasions, like a black-tie wedding or for the date with George Clooney...in my dreams.

Gigantor huge.

Low-budge or low-b short for low budget. Something that doesn't break the bank and allows you to pay your rent or mortgage at the end of the month.

Lurve When love can't fully describe the affection for something. Also from my fave film *Annie Hall*.

Martha as in Martha Stewart. Someone who is a crafty maven in the essence of the craft queen, Ms. Stewart.

Ne c'est pas French, meaning "is it not." Everything sounds chic-er in French.

Nekkid a more fun way of saying naked.

Pouffy sleeves that have a mind of their own and look like someone filled them with helium.

Puppy I call lots o' stuff puppies, from vintage dresses to needles to actual cute dogs.

Sesh short for session. I tend to over-abbreviate.

Sew-phobic those afraid of sewing or sewing machines

Zhuzhing giving a garment a little extra primping. I believe Carson Kressley got this into my vernacular during the *Queer Eye for the Straight Guy* era.

new dress a day

chapter one

SEWING 101

hese are sewing's basic moves, moves I learned in middle school while hammering out a teal sweatshirt **(yes, teal)** and humming Boyz II Men **("Although we've come . . . to the end of the rooooad . . . ")**.

In practicing these basics, grab your needles and thread and make sure you've got lots of light **(and a good playlist on in the background)** (see p. 123). Working at a desk or dining room table where you can set out your needles and spools of thread is ideal; however, you can couch it as long as you don't have butterfingers! Hidden needles in the upholstery are no-body's picnic. **(Tush + needles = a bloodcurdling scream rivaling Janet Leigh's in _Psycho_.)**

hand sewing

If you're one of those people who say, "but I can't even sew a button," prepare to remove that excuse from your vocabulary. With just some needles, a little bit of thread, and the ability to tie a knot, you can hand sew your little heart out!

There are a bunch of different kinds of stitches that you can learn, but we'll begin with the easiest and most useful **(in my humble opinion)**—the top three I use all the time.

Running stitch: Prepare to master this basic stitch in no time—easy, breezy, and doable for anyone.

1. Grab a piece of thread. I usually trim thread longer than necessary because it's better to have too much than not enough and run out before you're done. A good amount to keep in mind is about 1.5 to 2 times the length of the piece you need to stitch. Tie a knot at one end and take the other end and thread it through the eye of a needle.

2. Bring the needle up through the underside of the fabric (the knot will let you know when to stop). Bring the needle back down about ⅛ inch away from your first point.

3. Begin stitching from right to left, with evenly spaced stitches. The spacing between these stitches should be small, technically, but you can eyeball about ⅛ inch between stitches—do what works for you and the piece.

4. Repeat Steps 2 and 3 until a seam is finished, a hole is mended, or you want to take a snack break to Yogurtland.

a BASTING STITCH

is virtually the same as a running stitch, but with lots more room between the stitches. Basting stitches are used mostly as a temporary fix or hold, as they're easy to remove.

Backstitch: This stitch is one of the strongest, great at keeping seams together—meaning you won't have to worry about your pants tearing at the seam again when you drop your phone for the hundredth time.

> This happened to me and I didn't have anything to tie around my waist. Two words. Epic. Fail.

I think of this stitch as drawing an ocean wave—it goes forward, then back a little, then forward more, and back a little more.

1. Bring a threaded needle up through the underside of the fabric. Bring the needle back down 1 inch forward from where the needle came through.
2. Bringing your needle backward through the underside of the fabric in the middle of the stitch that was made, go another inch forward and bring the needle back down through the fabric.
3. Now bring your needle backward through the underside of the fabric again (in the middle of the last stitch) and make another stitch forward.
4. Continue this forward, backward, forward, backward movement until the seam has been stitched up.

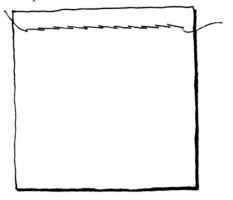

Overcast stitch: There's nothing foggy about this stitch, **(insert drum badump-ump here,)** which is perfect for sewing appliqués or fabric on tank tops. The zigzaggy overcast stitch is my favorite for putting patches or felted shapes on outfits because it gives a total handmade look.

1. Bring the needle through the underside of the fabric and bring it back down about ½ inch through the top of the fabric, on a slant.
2. Bring the needle back through the fabric from underneath and continue until you're through. With each stitch continue to move along the edge of the fabric, progressing farther along as you go.
3. Continue making diagonal stitches along the outside edges of your fabric or appliqué, and back through the fabric.

> It'll look like a pine tree/feather you drew in elementary school.

machine sewing

Sewing machines can be daunting if you've never used one. However, when you become one with the machine, you'll be hanging out and having cocktail hour together.

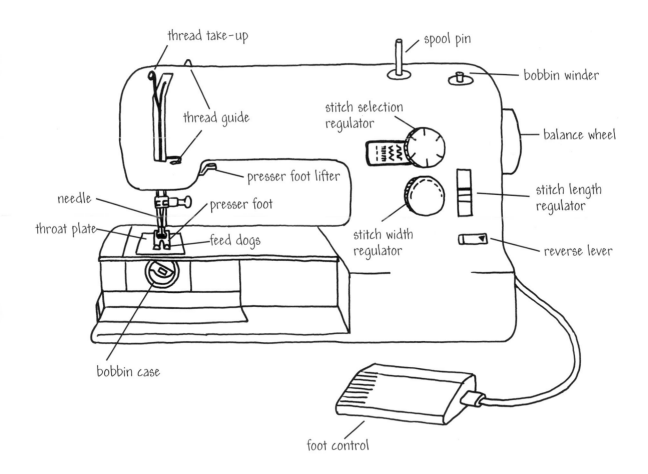

thread take-up

spool pin

bobbin winder

thread guide

stitch selection regulator

balance wheel

presser foot lifter

needle

presser foot

stitch length regulator

throat plate

feed dogs

stitch width regulator

reverse lever

bobbin case

foot control

Beginner machines: All the major brands—Elna, Brother, Kenmore, and Singer—make great machines for beginners, from mechanical to electronic and computerized—it's like Max Headroom is running the machine! You don't have to spend a lot either—many are under a hundred dollars! Head to retailers like Target or Walmart for a brand-new one, or scope out Craigslist for deals from people getting rid of the machines collecting dust in their attics.

If you're nervous about jumping into a sewing machine purchase, or want to test the waters first, sign up for a sewing class at a local community college or sewing store. They'll have a machine (and a teacher) to help you get comfortable before you decide to throw down Benjamins and buy your own.

Machine stitches: Each sewing machine gives you a bunch of different options to choose from:

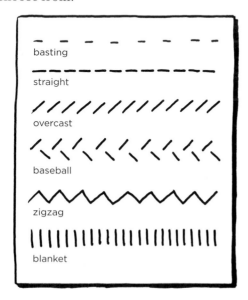

basting

straight

overcast

baseball

zigzag

blanket

The straight stitch is the one I use most often and it is exactly what it sounds like. Straight stitches in a row, forming a line across the fabric.

The zigzag stitch is perfect for attaching patches for a homemade look, making buttonholes, sewing stretch material, or even creating free-form letters. This stitch looks just like the front of Charlie Brown's shirt.

There's another zigzag stitch, the three-step zigzag stitch **(not to be confused with a square-dance move),** that looks similar to the zigzag stitch just mentioned. This stitch is most ideal for elastics or jersey knit because the zigzags are wider, giving more room for stretch and movement.

The blind hem stitch works as an invisible (kind of like Patrick Swayze in *Ghost*) stitch, perfect for hemming curtains or a skirt bottom. It's a mix of straight and zigzag stitches.

Many machines also include decorative stitches (like the blanket stitch, satin stitch, or whip stitch) for those who want to showcase their super-excellent sewing skills with fancy monograms.

Machine stitch lengths: Just like the saying: "Liquor before beer, you're in the clear; beer before liquor makes you sicker," I came up with a line for cautioning about stitch lengths:

"Short and sweet with no repeats;
long and loose probably reproduce."

This reminds me that the shorter the stitch the more durable it will be **(hopefully you won't have to sew it more than once),** and the longer the stitch the greater the likelihood you'll have to redo it. Stitch lengths will range from less than 1 to 6 millimeters, or 4 to 24 stitches per inch (these are the two scales of measurement). Looking at lengths, finer fabrics (satin) will be 1 or 2 mm; medium-thick fabric (cotton, linen) will stay right in the center at a length of 2.5 or 3 mm; and thicker fabrics (denim, corduroy) will be 4 or 5 mm.

Machine needles (also see "Needles" on p. xvi): Choosing the right needles for sewing different fabrics is like wearing the right clothes for each season. In summer you wear lighter clothing (and less of it), while in winter you wear layers of thicker clothing. Likewise, the thinner your fabric, the smaller the needle you'd use. Machine needles are sized "60/8" (smallest) to "120/19" (largest), with the first number associated with the diameter of the needle's shaft multiplied by 100 and the second number associated with the U.S. measuring system.

Bobbins (also see "Bobbins" on p. xv): Bobbins are a necessity for the sewing machine. A bobbin is to a spool of thread as Kid Sister is to My Buddy. **Sorry if I got that commercial jingle stuck in any of your heads.** They are mini spools that the thread is wound around beneath the throat plate inside the machine. The throat plate creates the stitches on the underside of the garment when sewing—the thread from the spool makes the top stitches—and without bobbins, the machine is just a big rectangular paperweight.

Wind That Bobbin!

1. Pick your thread and put it on the spool holder.
2. Take an empty bobbin and put it on the bobbin winder.
3. Pull the thread to the left and wrap it around the tension disk once, bringing it toward the bobbin winder on the right.
4. Wrap the thread clockwise around the bobbin a few times or bring the thread through the pinhole in the top of the bobbin, depending on the kind of bobbin you're using. Place the bobbin on the winding spindle.
5. Push the bobbin winder (with the bobbin on it) to the right until you hear the winder click in place.
6. Begin to press the foot pedal and the bobbin will spin, winding thread around it.
7. I like to have full bobbins, so continue to press the foot pedal until the bobbin is almost completely wound with thread. Some machines automatically stop when the bobbin is full, but if your machine doesn't, keep an eye on it at the ¾ point and stop it before it overflows at the bobbin's edge. You want the thread as smoothly wound as possible.

For additional tips on using a sewing machine see chapter 2: Muumuu Transformations, Option 1 (pp. 13–15). And remember, all sewing machines work differently, so refer to your machine manual for more detailed instructions.

chapter two

muumuu
TRANSFORMATIONS

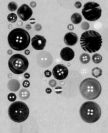rs. Roper, Homer Simpson, Erykah Badu: What do these folks have in common? They've all famously rocked a muumuu at some point. I'm all about vegging out in this shapeless robe/nightgown/cloth dress in the privacy of my apartment, but I won't leave the house in one unless I've done a little bit of mending first. Scratch that, a *lot* of mending.

To ring in my thirtieth birthday, I transformed my first frockish muumuu from drab to fab. The celebratory outfit kicked off my year of new pieces, and I pulled it off with little more than a pair of scissors and some cinching!

The main essence of this remake was going from long to short, a totally easy fix on a too-long garment or a muumuu plucked from an estate sale at an Edie Beale look-alike's home.

This is an easy starting point for all levels, so all you non-sewers out there, get ready for your mind to be blown because you'll be able to nail this in a jiffy too!

look #1

machine it muumuu

Dressipe

- **Muumuu**
- **Chalk, pencil, or a fabric crayon**
- **Ruler (or straightedge object)**
- **Scissors**
- **Iron**
- **Straight pins**
- **Thread**
- **Sewing machine**

If you are using a sewing machine, continue the steps below. If you are hand sewing, skip to p. 20.

1. Decide how short to go. Pick your desired length and, using chalk, a pencil, or a fabric crayon, mark the muumuu where you want it to end. Remember to use your ruler or phone book, or other straight marking device to create a straight line. This line will be your guide as you snip, snip, snip across the fabric.

2. Cut about 1 to 2 inches below your marked line. This will be the excess material to assist with your hem. Also, keep those trimmings because you'll use them later.

3. Now that the piece has been cut, plug in an iron. Fold the piece under at the chalk line and use the iron to press down, making a crease along the line. Continue ironing the fabric along the chalk line, making your way around the piece.

4. Now it's time to do it all again!

I know, I know, we had so much fun the first time.

Fold the raw edge in half (raw edge is folded under, touching the wrong side of the fabric) all the way around the dress, and again, use the iron to press down on the new crease, getting it super flat.

5. As you iron, pin the folded fabric in place. This will keep everything you've pressed from moving or coming undone.

6. Once the garment is pressed and pinned, a sewing machine makes creating a hem super easy. Pick your thread and use it to wind a bobbin (see "Wind That Bobbin" on p. 9). Lace up your sewing machine with that same thread and put in your bobbin!

7. Adjust your machine to the appropriate stitch setting. With a cotton muumuu like this, a medium stitch, 2.5 mm to 3 mm, will work the best (see "Machine Stitch Lengths" on p. 8).

8. Lift the presser foot and slide the bottom of your garment (where the hem is pinned) underneath the presser foot of the sewing machine, right side up.

9. Align the garment with the $5/8$ mark on the throat plate, which is a good hem allotment. Feel free to choose whatever amount you're happy with, as there is no right or wrong, and put the presser foot back down.

10. Use the handwheel to stitch forward 3 or 4 stitches.

11. Then press down the reverse lever and go backward a few stitches, directly on top of what you just stitched. This backward and forward action reinforces your stitches so that everything stays in place before you get farther along. After sewing forward, then backward, begin stitching forward again and continue stitching along. You can do this once more for extra security—there is no right or wrong.

12. After your first stitches are secure, slowly slide the rest of your fabric along the throat plate, using the $^5/_8$ seam allotment mark (or whichever seam measurement you chose) as a guide.

13. As you reach the place where you began your stitches, repeat Steps 11 and 12, going backward and forward over your last stitches to keep them in place.

14. Use the reserved material you cut in Step 2 and trim it more if desired to use as a belt, gathering your muumuu at the waist. (At least 1-inch wide will cinch the waist without being obvious, and a wider piece will make the fabric more beltish-looking.)

You now have a gorgeous hem and matching cinch-erific belt, and your muumuu transformation is complete!

look #2

CUT & GO!

Dressipe

- **Muumuu**
- **Chalk, pencil, or a fabric crayon**
- **Ruler (or straightedge object)**
- **Scissors**

 Non-sewers, you've got a few options to create the same look without using a machine.

If you're working with a polyester blend, leaving the edges raw is a perfectly fine option. Just make sure your snips are straight.

Leave the jagged edges to Glenn Close and Jeff Bridges.

1. Follow Step 1 on p. 13 to mark your desired length.

2. Use scissors to cut your piece along the marked line. Straight snips = fab post-cut muumuu!

3. Using the leftover material, cut another strip (at least 1-inch wide), and you've got an insta-belt!

Fastest. Dress. Ever.

look #3

tape & shake

Dressipe

- **Muumuu**
- **Chalk, pencil, or a fabric crayon**
- **Ruler (or straightedge object)**
- **Scissors**
- **Iron**
- **Tape (mailing, duct, painter's, or Gorilla Tape)**

Nothing beats a quick hem with the use of some mailing, painter's, or duct tape to secure the ends.

1. Follow Steps 1 and 2 on p. 13 to mark your desired length plus about 1 to 2 inches for a hem fold.

2. Post-trim, if you've got a bit of fraying, turn to that "everything drawer" in the kitchen that's filled with spare keys, tape, and take-out menus from Baja Fresh, and go for that tape.

3. Fold your garment, and using a hot iron to press down on the fold, make your way around the piece.

4. Grab your tape and place it evenly over the frayed ends, securing it to the underside of the dress.

Easy, breezy!

look #4

STITCH & no BITCH

Dressipe

- **Muumuu**
- **Chalk, pencil, or a fabric crayon**
- **Ruler (or straightedge object)**
- **Scissors**
- **Iron**
- **Straight pins**
- **Thread**
- **Hand needle**

If you are flying around the world on work trips, here's where that travel sewing kit in the Marriott bathroom finally comes in handy! Using a needle from the kit as well as one of the threads that matches the color of your piece, a basic running stitch will do the trick.

1. Follow Steps 1 and 2 on p. 13 to mark your desired length plus about 1 to 2 inches for a hem fold.

2. Grab a piece of thread. Estimating thread length is always a bit tricky. I always eyeball it depending on the length of the piece I'm working with, and, of course, no two dresses are ever the same. Because you don't want to have a piece of thread that runs out, overestimate it. Tie a knot at one end and push the other end through the eye of a medium-size needle.

3. Bring the needle up through the underside of the fabric (the knot will let you know when to stop). Bring the needle back down about 1/8 inch away from your first point.

4. Begin stitching from right to left, with evenly spaced stitches. The spacing between these stitches should be small, technically, but you can eyeball about 1/8 inch between each one—do what works for you and the piece.

5. When you get back to the starting point, knot the thread several times at the end to keep it in place.

Shortened muumuu/ house dress is dunzo!

TYPICAL HEM ALLOTMENTS

I don't use set measurements for everything—I think it all depends on the fabric. For a thicker fabric, I would use a 5/8- or 3/4-inch; however, with thinner fabrics, like cotton, it can be much less, like 1/4 inch. There are easy lines to follow on the throat plate of the sewing machine (underneath the presser foot); just follow the lines on your machine to your liking and you'll be fine.

chapter three

TWO-MINUTE TUNICS

I'm a T-shirt-and-jeans kind of gal, and I live in my flip-flops most of the year, thanks to the glorious Southern California climate. On those days when a little more effort needs to be given **(i.e., date nights or a girlfriend's birthday dinner, or evenings when Marisa trades the Havaianas for some heels)**, I like to go the jeans-and-nice-top route. Tunics rule in my book; paired with denim or tights, they create a chic look that happens to be super comf, and you don't have to worry about sucking in your stomach after that big meal **(plus birthday cake)**. With its Roman roots, the tunic is a flowy staple in my closet that always makes me feel put-together. **I would have lurved living during the Roman Empire, solely for the drapey duds and gladiator sandals.** A sneaky trick? Absolutely. But going for that extra bite of crème brûlée without worrying about feeling restricted by my clothes is most definitely worth it.

mexican tunic

Dressipe

- **Muumuu/Dress**
- **Chalk, pencil, or a fabric crayon**
- **Ruler (or straightedge object)**
- **Scissors**
- **Iron**
- **Straight pins**
- **Thread**
- **Sewing machine or hand needle (sew option)**
- **Tape (no-sew option)**

(For step-by-step images see "Muumuu Transformations" on pp. 11–21.)

Using chapter 2 as a guide, we're going to do the same thing for this tunic that we did for the muumuus. And whichever hem option (machine sewn, hand sewn, or taped) suits you best will work. In this case, my piece is made of very thin cotton, which will fray pretty soon after trimming, so leaving the edges raw won't work.

1. Decide how short to go. Pick your desired length and mark the tunic where you want it to end using your choice of writing utensil. Remember to use something with a straight edge (ruler, yardstick, or phone book) for a straight line. This line will be your guide as you trim away across the fabric.

2. Cut about 1 to 2 inches below your marked line. This will be the excess material to assist with your hem. Don't throw away those trimmings—keep them for later use!

3. Now that the piece has been cut, plug in an iron. Fold the piece under at the chalk line, press down with the iron, making a crease along the line. Continue ironing the fabric along the chalk line, making your way around the piece.

4. Now it's time to do it all again! Fold the raw edge in half (raw edge should be folded under, touching the wrong side of the fabric) all the way around the tunic, and again, press down on the new crease with the iron, getting it super flat.

5. As you iron, pin the folded fabric in place. This will keep everything you've pressed from moving or coming undone.

6. Once the garment is pressed and pinned, a sewing machine makes creating a hem easy. Pick your thread and use it to wind a bobbin. (See "Wind That Bobbin" on p. 9.) If you are using a sewing machine, continue the steps below. If you are hand sewing, skip to step 14. If

you are using tape, skip to step 15.

7. Thread your sewing machine and put in your bobbin.

8. Adjust your machine to the appropriate stitch settings. With super-thin material like this sheer cotton, a 2-mm stitch will work the best. (See "Machine Stitch Lengths" on pp. 8–9.)

9. Lift the presser foot, slide the bottom of the garment underneath it, and line the garment at the $5/8$ mark on the throat plate. Put the presser foot back down.

10. Use the handwheel to stitch forward 3 or 4 stitches.

11. Press down the reverse lever and go backward a few stitches, directly on top of what you just stitched, before sewing forward again and continuing along. This backward and forward action reinforces your stitches so that everything stays in place before you get to the nitty-gritty of the piece.

12. After your first stitches are secure, slowly slide the rest of your fabric along the throat plate, using the $5/8$-inch seam allotment (or whichever seam you chose on the throat plate) as a guide.

13. As you reach the place where you began your stitches, repeat Steps 10 and 11, going backward and forward over your last stitches to keep them in place.

14. To hand sew, pick desired thread, trim an amount $1^1/_2$ times the length of the hem, and tie a knot at one end of the thread. Thread your needle and begin a running stitch around the bottom of the tunic to create a new hem.

15. If you're using tape, tape down the hem from the underside of the tunic.

Tunic, jeans, and espadrille wedges scream margarita party time, don'tcha think?

red, white, and blue with buttons

Dressipe

- **Muumuu/dress**
- **Chalk, pencil, or a fabric crayon**
- **Ruler (or straightedge object)**
- **Scissors**
- **Seam ripper**
- **Thread**
- **Hand needles or safety pins**

For this nautical tunic, all I needed was a trim across. I went with the cut-and-done method, leaving the edges raw because this thick polyester material was unlikely to unravel or roll up at the edges.

1. Choose your desired length and mark it (I chose mid-thigh). Using scissors, cut a straight line across.

2. Remove any unwanted embellishments. (I removed the buttons on the torso with a seam ripper. You can use scissors as well to take them off.)

3. Use safety pins to affix any embellishments you'd like, especially if they're temporary. When done carefully, this can be a solid fix, but stitching down buttons and appliqués helps them stay in place permanently.

4. Here I took three of the removed buttons and sewed them in a pattern mirroring the one already found on the top of the piece.

removing EMBELLISHMENTS

When removing buttons or appliqués, just be careful to only clip the threads attaching the pieces to the garment. Lack of attention might lead to holes—yikes!

The tunic paired with opaque tights works just as well as with jeans, so have fun switching it up!

chapter four
sundresses

I'm "Walking On Sunshine" (ohhh) because it's "Summertime" and the livin' is easy. Sure, it's easy to stay cool with a "Summer Breeze" when the thermometer hits triple digits; otherwise it's just a (cruel) "Cruel Summer." Sure, "Some Like It Hot," but when "The Heat Is On" you need to don just the right piece to deal with the "Heat Wave" or fear turning into a "Blister in the Sun." Before you start "Burning Up" with a "Fever" and have to wear those "Sunglasses at Night," here's a recipe for a dress that won't make you feel like you're in a "Ring of Fire" anymore.

Modern-day Fresh Prince? Yeah, I know, I'm sticking to my day job . . .

Growing up in New York, as soon as the first glimmer of summer appeared, it was shorts and sandals all the way. It may have been only 60 degrees out, but to us summer was already in full swing. Goodbye to months of dark winter mornings, putting on rough and starchy jeans that felt like sandpaper, turning on the car to let it warm up and defrost the windshields twenty minutes before leaving the house. And let's be honest, my legs were in hibernation mode **(aka I wouldn't shave for weeks),** so bringing dresses back into the mix was a pretty splendid thing.

Now that I live in Los Angeles, I don't have to experience this anymore. But the memories feel as if it was just yesterday. **I literally just got the chills!** And my love of sundresses is as strong as ever.

look #1

RIBBON STRAP DRESS

Dressipe

- **Skirt with elastic band**
- **A bit of trim**—You'll want enough to make straps out of the lace, elastic, fringe, ribbon, etc. that you use, so measure accordingly. I used 8 inches for each cotton strap, so I made sure to have a foot and a half just in case extra was needed. You'll use more or less, depending on length needed and the stretch of the fabric.
- **Ruler (or straightedge object)**
- **Scissors**
- **Straight pins**
- **Sewing machine, or hand needle, and thread (sew option)**
- **Safety pins (no-sew option)**

One of my favorite sundress styles involves an elastic skirt. Not only is it comfortable to wear, it's beyond easy to make and can be finished in a cinch. Scope out your own closet and you just may find the perfect base for crafting this cool and breezy creation. All you need is a skirt with an elastic band and a bit of trim—any sort of trim will work for this (lace, elastic, fringe, or ribbon)—just have fun and get creative because there is no wrong choice.

1. Put on the elastic skirt and pull it up over your chestal area to the exact point you want the dress to sit.

2. Pin the trim in place to the front and back of the skirt at each shoulder, making straps.

3. Once the trim is pinned on both sides of the dress, stitch all four edges in place. A straight stitch on the machine or a running stitch by hand will suffice. Go over each edge a few times to strengthen the stitch and to keep it from coming undone. Test stitches' strength by pulling the straps to make sure they feel secure. If they give a little, then it's a sign that you should stitch edges a few more times. To go the no-sew route, use safety pins to keep the straps in place, pinning each edge to the dress.

4. Grab a belt to cinch at the waist or let it billow away in the summer breezes.

Dress done! Time to shave the legs.

GOING STRAPLESS/SLEEVELESS

I'm a big fan of going strapless. There is just something about the nekkid collarbone that I adore. Maybe it's the leotards I wore for years of ballet, the costumes with thin elastic straps, our focus on keeping our shoulders pushed down while we moved from first to fifth position doing pliés and échappés; and it's just ingrained in my noggin. Maybe it's the nostalgia of watching Madonna flaunt a strapless pink taffeta gown like Marilyn in her "Material Girl" video on MTV as a kid, which, of course, made me want a pink dress and a crew of tuxedoed gentlemen to carry me around in it. Same goes for ZZ Top's "Legs" vid because I was obsessed with all those shoes!

Whatever the reason, I've come to love the way a strapless dress works, and I tend to go this route when in doubt. Showing off a little shoulder never hurt anyone, right? For those a little shy in showing off both deltoid muscles, baby steps can be taken before going full frontal (in the shoulder department) with an asymmetrical style dress.

Kind of perfect for the beginner or the novice, *ne c'est pas*?

look #2

STRAPLESS DRESS

Dressipe

- **Dress**
- **Scissors**
- **Straight pins**
- **Thread**
- **Sewing machine or hand needle**
- **Safety pin**

1. Trim a straight line across the top of the dress, cutting right below the arms or an area that will garner enough material to cover the boobs! This doesn't have to be perfect because the raw edges will be pinned under and mistakes hidden. Set aside the arm remnants for later use.

2. Begin pinning the raw edge of the dress under. Make sure you leave about $3/4$ inch between the top of the dress and where you pin, because you will later add a drawstring to this area.

3. Once the edges are completely pinned down, time to stitch in place. Use either a running stitch by hand or a straight stitch using a sewing machine to bind them together.

4. Now that you've stitched your top seam, snip a slit up top, in the center, and vertically within the seam on the front of the dress. This is going to be where the drawstring is inserted.

5. From the reserved arm remnants, trim about ½-inch strips (try to make them straight if you can) and stitch together the ends to act as the drawstring. Make sure the drawstring is long enough to fit around your bust and there's enough to make a bow at the end. If the dress doesn't have long sleeves or you don't have enough fabric, use ribbon instead.

6. Put a safety pin through one end of your drawstring and push it through the slit made in Step 4. Use the safety pin to guide and push the drawstring through the space in the seam until it makes a full trip around and comes out on the other side.

7. Once the drawstring has come out on the other side, remove the safety pin, put the dress on, tie a bow in the front, and your strapless piece is complete.

Watch out Madge, there's a new material girl in town!

look #3

asymmetrical dress

Dressipe

- **Dress**
- **Chalk, pencil, fabric crayon, or straight pins to mark**
- **Ruler (or straightedge object)**
- **Scissors**
- **Thread**
- **Sewing machine or hand needle**

When I saw this dress with what looked like claws on the shoulder, it roared (pun!) asymmetrical. I wanted to make the brown material the focal point, and taking off the left side of the dress would make that happen.

1. Before getting scissor happy, try on the dress to see where it falls—pay special attention to covering up the boobal area. Use pins or chalk to mark the 45-degree line across the chest where you want the dress to fall.

2. Leaving an extra ½ inch to have on reserve for folding under and stitching, use scissors to snip along the diagonal line you created. If, like mine, your dress has a zipper,

when cutting across, make sure that the zipper's slider is pulled down to the bottom stop, so you don't trim it off.

3. Pin under the ½ inch of reserved material with raw edges.

4. Use a running stitch to sew a new top seam. (If your dress has a zipper, start sewing on the right side of the zipper and stitch completely around until you reach the left side of the zipper.)

If you have a zipper, hand stitch the ends of the zipper and the teeth down—we want to make sure the slider stays in place and the zipper doesn't pop off, so sewing on top of the zipper is key.

5. Try on the dress once more to check for any problem areas. In my dress, the extra fabric draping on the left side would cause some flashing issues if left as is, so I took it in 2 inches to fit. I turned the dress inside out, pinned the 2 inches that needed tightening, and sewed by machine a quick straight stitch to keep it in place. This can also be tackled with a running stitch by hand. Once the area was

sewed, I trimmed off the excess material and returned the dress to the right side.

Always feel free to add elastic or a ribbon strap to keep the dress in place if you're nervous that it might fall. To do this, use the same technique in Ribbon Strap Dress (pp. 33–34).

Get ready girls, it's strapless bra time.

TOPSTICK

The most prized trick in the book is using Topstick as double-stick tape. It's made for toupees and will keep everything tacked down, especially slinky material over the décolletage, preventing nip slips! If only George Costanza used it in "The Beard" episode of *Seinfeld*, Elaine would never have been able to pull off his toupee!

chapter five

TWeaKs on
THe BaSICS

op quiz, hot shot: Who's got two thumbs and a slew of sweatshirts, T-shirts, and jeans that just sit in sweater boxes below her bed? This girl!

How hot did Jennifer Beals make a plain old sweatshirt look in *Flashdance?* How many plain old sweatshirts do I have in my drawers that look anywhere close to that hot? None. Zero. Zilch . . . until now. I don't really *need* to own seventeen sweatshirts that virtually fit me the same way. This remake is going to garner me a completely new sweatshirt, one that is meant for a bucket of water to be dropped on it. **Cue Irene Cara's "What a Feeling" and let's get started.**

look #1

sweatshirt

Dressipe

- **Old sweatshirt**
- **Scissors**
- **Straight pins**
- **Thread**
- **Sewing machine or hand needle**

Let's take an old college sweatshirt I procured from an ex-boyfriend, from a school I didn't attend, and cut it up like Edward Scissorhands! The kicker with this one: The inside fleece is going to be the new outside of the sweatshirt!

1. Cut the ribbed neck first. This doesn't have to be a drastic snip, just enough to take off the neck. Take off a little or a lot, depending on how much shoulder you want to show. It's easier to cut if you follow the ribbed neck as a guide, so begin on one side, either left or right, and cut around the neck to the other side. Do the same with the sleeves and cut off the ribbed cuffs.

2. If your sweatshirt is a bit oversized and you'd like it to be more fitted, you can take in the waist and arms. (My sweatshirt was an XXL and I wanted it to be slimmer, so I followed these steps.) Try on

the sweatshirt and pinch the material at your torso and arms that you want to get rid of and place pins in these spots to use as markers for where you'll sew. If you have a friend around to help, let them be your personal assistant and pin the spots for you. If your sweatshirt fits perfectly, then skip to Step 5.

3. Take off the sweatshirt and mark the area that was just pinned with a Sharpie or chalk line. This is what you'll follow when you make your stitches. Do this on the top/logo side of the sweatshirt, because after it's stitched it will be turned inside out since the fleece interior is your new exterior.

4. Stitch the arms and the torso area over the pins on the top side of the fabric with either a straight machine stitch or running hand stitch.

5. Trim the excess sweatshirt material by following the seam (leave about a ½ inch).

6. Turn sweatshirt inside out and put it on.

Insta-J. Beals.

denim skirt

Dressipe

- **Denim jeans**
- **Chalk, pencil, or a fabric crayon**
- **Ruler (or straightedge object)**
- **Scissors**
- **Seam ripper**
- **Straight pins**
- **Thread**
- **Sewing machine or hand needle**

I live in jeans. They're the staple wardrobe item I just can't live without. What I can live without are the thirty pairs that I currently own. Do I still need that denim Bisou Bisou jumpsuit I bought in 1999? No! Do I need bedazzled pocketed Sevens from the mid 2000s? No! Those black Calvin Kleins from high school still get a wear every now and again, so they stay. But do I need those old Wranglers that I bought at a thrift store just because they were Wranglers? No! I love the versatility of denim and how it really can go with anything. For those pairs that you may not wear all the time, but that still deserve a little love, this easy remake will keep the top part of them around while saving some room in your closet.

1. Take a pair of those old jeans (I grabbed those previously mentioned Wranglers) and cut them into shorts. Keep in mind that the length you choose to cut your shorts will be about the same length of the skirt. If you cut Daisy Dukes, you're going to have a mini, mini denim skirt, so be wary! If you want to leave the edges raw, cut the jeans at exactly the length of your choosing, but if you want to hem the bottom, leave an extra inch when snipping.

2. Remove the seam from the crotch and thigh area with a seam ripper on the front and back of the jeans, opening up the entire bottom, beginning right below the zipper.

3. Lay your jeans completely flat on your work surface and begin working on the front. Overlap the crotch pieces so the right side fits flat underneath the left side. Take a swatch of denim leftover from what was cut off in Step 1 and pin this to the center of the overlapped denim from underneath.

4. Turn the piece over and repeat Step 3 for the back of the jeans.

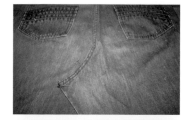

5. Once the front and back have been pinned down, it's time to stitch everything in place. Pay close attention to the thread color used elsewhere in the jeans and do your best to match it. The threads are usually shades of blue; however, some jeans are stitched with other colors. In my case, they were stitched with red thread.

While a sewing machine is quickest for this task, this can easily be hand stitched as well.

That was what I did in college when I had no sewing machine.

Lace up your sewing machine with your desired thread color and set the stitch length to a 4 or 5 since denim, a thicker fabric, is being used. Leave the pins in the garment and remove them as you sew over them. Stitch the front and back areas in place.

6. Once the front and back are stitched, it's time to focus on the bottom of the skirt. If you're not going to hem the skirt, it will already be near your desired length, so trim around the edges (just to even and straighten the areas where the crotch overlapped) and enjoy the frayed look. For sewing a hem, trim around the edges to even out the bottom, fold 1 inch under, pin in place, and stitch around.

New denim skirt from a pair of old jeans, total score!

crafternooning

Schedule craft-ernoons (my favorite days—craft afternoons) with your girlfriends. Sharing paints, brushes, and stencils will lower the cost of this project even more (could be less than a grande drip coffee from Starbucks).

look #3

OLD T-SHIRT transformation

Dressipe

- **Solid-color short- or long-sleeved T-shirt**
- **Stencils (I used Tulip Adhesive-Backed Stencils.)**
- **Scissors**
- **Paper grocery bag or cutting board—something flat to put in the middle of the T-shirt while painting**
- **Fabric paint (I used Tulip Fashion Glitter Shimmer Fabric Paint.)**
- **Painting utensil (I used Q-tips)**

Now, I have my favorite tees (the vintage Dos Equis tee I found for fifty cents at a garage sale in Westwood and the Justified tee from Justin Timberlake's inaugural album launch party hold a special place in my heart), but there are the others that don't really see the light of day. They're soft, they're comfortable, but they're in constant hibernation. Those are going to be transformed into pieces that will make the leap from under the bed to dresser drawer status.

1. Grab a blank T-shirt from your collection; one in a school color or just basic white or black Hanes tee.

2. Insert a large, folded paper grocery bag or cutting board into the middle of the shirt.

3. Cut and affix your favorite stencils to the tee.

Put a name, a school mascot, or whatever tickles your fancy. I chose my alma mater and placed a U, S, and C.

hour. Repeat this until you achieve your desired shade.

5. Once your final coat of paint has thoroughly dried (I let my tee dry overnight to be safe), peel off the stencils.

The new tee is ready for the big game! (Fight on Trojans!) We've got spirit, yes we do. We've got spirit, how about you?

4. Once stencils are down, select a fabric paint and use a foam brush (or any brushing device—I went to my bathroom cabinet for a Q-tip) to dab the areas inside the stencil. Coat once with paint and let it dry for at least 1 hour. Apply another coat of paint and let it dry for an additional

PAINTBRUSH OPTIONS

I like using wood-handled sponge brushes because they tend to leave a smoother finish, but any craft paintbrush will work. Kitchen sponges and even Q-tips will do the trick if you don't have any brushes close by, but keep in mind that the cotton may unravel and become stringy.

chapter six

DESIGNER
LOOK-ALIKES

It's no secret that I'm a total bargain girl when it comes to fashion. I was obsessed with Style Network's *The Look for Less* with Elisabeth Hasselbeck back in 2002 when she was still Elisabeth Filarski. It was my favorite show concept: Take a high-end piece from the runways of Vera Wang or Prada and make a low-budge version on the cheap. I love watching *Access Hollywood* and all those red-carpet shows before awards ceremonies too. **(I'm pretty much glued to E! all day on Oscar Sunday.)** It's fun to critique my favorite celebs so I can try to create my own version of those very expensive pieces without going overboard!

In trying to re-create your fave celebs' style, or couture straight from the runways of Paris, always keep a few key elements in mind when you're out and about.

Color: Keep your eyes peeled for color. If you can match the same pink as Reese Witherspoon's Monique Lhullier wedding dress in something equally as cocktaily, then you've got the perfect base to start off with in copying the blushing bride look.

Pattern: Look for something with a similar pattern. If you want to rock the same leopard-ish style as Gwen Stefani or Mary-Kate Olsen, scour racks with an animal print in mind. Maybe you won't find the same dress, but you might come across a top that gets the essence of the No Doubt-er or a scarf similar to the Full Hous-er. You can rock it with the same bling necklace, plunging neckline, or red lips!

Fabric and Hardware: Fabric and hardware are key. If you love Katy Perry's dripping-in-sequins look, then glimmer should be on the radar. Look for pieces with similar beading, or even metallic fabric, to give off that same red-carpet shine on your own carpet. Then you can go a little crazy with rhinestones to add your own fireworks.

look #1

gucci purse

Dressipe

- **Purse**
- **Work space cover (newspaper, old towel, or sheet)**
- **Ribbon in shades of green and red (I used grosgrain.)**

- **Glue (I used Aleene's Fabric Fusion)**
- **Scissors**
- **Ruler, if desired**

I love how you can tell a brand just by looking at their logo. Louis Vuitton and Fendi have interlocking LVs and Fs, Polo Ralph Lauren has the horse and cute little jockey, and Gucci has the green and red stripes. For this remake, I found a purse at Goodwill with a similar shape to a vintage Gucci hobo bag—leather, zipper on top, and with a clean surface so that ribbons could be easily added. I then picked up grosgrain ribbons in shades of crimson and forest green to match Gucci's signature colors.

1. Cover your work surface with newspaper or an old towel to prevent glue from getting on your floor or table.

2. Apply fabric glue to the back of the crimson ribbon. Place the ribbon (adhesive side down) vertically at the center of the bag. (The line should be straight to truly mimic Gucci, so affix the top of the ribbon to the top of the purse first and then slowly work your way down the rest of the ribbon to seal it in place. Use a ruler for total perfection.)

3. Repeat Step 1 with two strips of green ribbon. Apply one strip to each side of the crimson ribbon.

4. Use scissors to cut the ends of the ribbon when you get to the bottom of the purse. You can also glue the ends under for a smooth finish if they're frayed. Just leave an extra $1/2$ inch where the ribbon meets the edge of the purse, dab an extra bit of glue on each side of this $1/2$ inch and fold under to secure.

Vintage bag with a hint of designer-ness made from the comforts of your home and just a fraction of the price tag.

TO BUY OR NOT TO BUY moments:

- Dress fits like a glove but has an asymmetrical tear from the hips down. **BUY!** Cut it and turn it into a top. (See chapter 3 for creating tunics!)
- You already have three similar pieces that look like this. **BUY NOT!** You don't really need a fourth.
- Dress can be turned into a staple LBD. **BUY!** (See chapter 19 for this LBD redo.)
- Garment reminds you of something you've seen in Elle. **BUY!** (See chapter 6 for designer look-alikes.)

versace JLo Dress

Dressipe

- **Dress with a similar cut to the designer piece**
- **Seam ripper**
- **Scissors**
- **Matching fabric (preferably something with stretch)**
- **Straight pins**
- **Sewing machine, or hand needle, and thread (sew option)**
- **Glue gun and glue sticks, or safety pins (no-sew option)**
- **Brooch**

This dress was instantly iconic when JLo wore it to the Grammys in 2000. The jungle-inspired fabric and deep, down to the waist V-neck made it über memorable. Trey Parker and Matt Stone mocked it on the Oscars' red carpet that year and Matt Lauer even found it as a Halloween costume and wore it on *Today*.

With a few liberties taken, a version of this dress isn't too difficult. The key part is finding the right material to tack on top of another dress with a similar cut. Here, the V-neck of this piece was easily removed (or partially removed to avoid an X-rating!). With a few key stitches and pins, the fabric can effortlessly hang on top of it.

1. Use a seam ripper to remove the stitches holding together the lace in the V-neck.

2. Next, to mimic the high slit, continue using the seam ripper to unstitch the front of the dress from the bottom to mid-thigh, or cut a slit with scissors to extend up to your thighs.

3. With the matching fabric that will cover the skirt part of the dress, take the center of the material and put it at the center of your back (right at your tailbone) and pull both sides around your body.

4. Pin the material to your waist, then pin the edges of the hanging material to the edges of the actual dress, going up the slit. The fabric will be drapey, so it doesn't have to be perfect when you're attaching.

5. With the dress still on, measure enough fabric to cover the area from the waist to the shoulders in front and from the shoulders to the tailbone in back. Make sure the width of the fabric is long enough to cover both arms too. Pin the material in place at the wrists and shoulders, then take off the dress.

6. With the material pinned to the shoulder seam, cut a slit down the center of the fabric to pin carefully to the inside of the V-neck.

This is guerrilla seamstressing at its finest—one of those "make it work" moments. It's basically all about making sure you cover the entire dress with the fabric however you can.

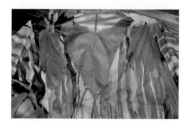

7. Pin down all the material on the front under the arms, at the waist, and cut a slit down the material in the back of the dress where the zipper lays, and pin each side of the material to each side of the zipper.

It's important to be able to zip this dress.

8. Pin down all the material to the back of the dress, at the tailbone, and on each side. Tuck the material underneath the separate skirt material at the waist. Let the excess fabric hanging under the arms just drape off.

9. Tack down the edges whichever way is easiest. If this is just a costume for a party, use a glue gun or safety pins. If you have time on a cross-country flight, use thread and needles. (Yes, they're TSA approved!) If time is of the essence and there is a sewing machine nearby, plug it in and get going. This is a "make it work" piece, so listen to that mantra and pick your poison.

10. After the fabric is glued or sewn, remove the pins, add a sparkly brooch at the waist, and a slicked-back ponytail to complete the outfit.

I'm still, I'm still Marisa from the block.

chanel dress

Dressipe

- **Scoop-neck dress**
- **Stencil (chain-link stencil found at Blick Art Materials)**
- **Gold paint (I used Tulip Fashion Glitter Shimmer Fabric Paint)**
- **Paintbrush (I used a foam brush. Check chapter 5: Old T-shirt Transformation for brush options)**
- **Tape (just a bit of duct tape to keep the dress in place)**
- **Work space cover (paper bag, newspaper, or old sheet)**

Chanel is iconic, from the quilted leather handbags, to the fragrances, to the inter-twined C insignia. I adore a particular red, vintage Chanel dress with actual chain links draped from it. I thrifted a basic red, scoop-neck dress with an open neckline to match the Chanel version, but there may even be a dress in your closet right now waiting for a little pick-me-up. Unfortunately, I couldn't go with real 24-karat gold for my piece *(gold is expensive, yo!),* so instead, I substituted chain-link stencils and gold paint—the next best thing.

1. Begin with covering your work surface with newspaper, grocery bags, or an old sheet that you won't care if paint gets on it. Lay the dress and tape the straps down to the work surface.

2. Use a chain-link stencil and tape the stencil edges to the dress along the neckline, starting with the left side. Use the neckline as your guide for where the stencil should be placed as you go along.

3. Use foam paintbrushes to apply the paint, dabbing it within the stencils. Let dry for at least 1 hour. Repeat Steps 2 and 3 until the neck is completely lined with painted chains.

Faux Chanel is complete.

SWAP PARTIES

Instead of thrifting one weekend, gather the girls for an afternoon swapping party! Everyone brings clothes they're tired of; the garments are hung on racks to shop through, and the gals go home with fabulous new duds. One friend's trash is another friend's treasure. Check out swap.com and TheSwapaholics.com for more ideas on online swapping and swap parties coming to your town, or hit up a local Buffalo Exchange, Crossroads Trading Co., Beacon's Closet, Wasteland, or Plato's Closet, where you can sell your used items for cash, or trade for other merch in the store.

chapter seven

DIY BLACK TIE

'm in the "all your friends are getting married" stage of my life right now, and let me tell you, it's a pretty penny! From gifts on the Tiffany registry (FYI, my registry will be with Target, y'all) to airplane tickets and rooms at the W; the last place I want to spend money is on something to wear.

Smack-dab in the middle of my year-long one-dollar-a-day vow, I received a lovely wedding invite stating the following: BLACK TIE.

Like Kim Novak in *Vertigo,* I spun, then the background spun, then I nearly fainted. I couldn't creep past the promise I made when I started the blog, but I didn't think there was any way to make a black-tie outfit for a dollar, and I didn't want to take more pictures with the same people in the same thing I wore when I last saw them, you know). Time to get creative! Can you DIY black tie? On a budget? Sure you can.

Off I went on the hunt for the perfect piece. One Sunday I woke up and did my usual—grabbed a handful of singles, drove through McDonald's for a vanilla iced coffee, scoured some garage sales/flea markets/big piles of throwaways, and I found a dress, I found *the* dress.

So, moral of the story—yes, you can! You can do red carpet with something that looks like the carpet of your car. Fancier dresses can be resurrected from ugly throwaways . . . here are a few examples to get your juices flowing!

red velvet dress

Dressipe

- **Dress**
- **Seam ripper**
- **Scissors**
- **Straight pins**
- **Sewing machine, or hand needle, and thread (sew option)**
- **Fabric glue (no-sew option)**

Unfortunately, this dress got stuck with Keanu Reeves in that phone booth/time machine in the '90s, and right now it's no excellent adventure. For dresses like this, think simplicity.

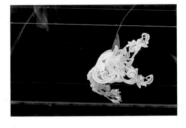

1. Use a seam ripper to remove any extra fabric or embellishments (like the lace and beaded collar).

2. Continue to use the seam ripper to carefully remove the seams connecting the strips attached to the neckband at the top of the dress.

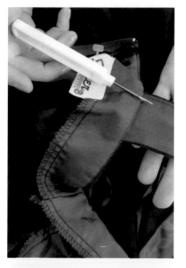

3. Pin down the top of the dress where the strips were removed and hand stitch the seam closed. Use an easy running stitch and go from one side to the other just to close up the opening.

If you want a floor-length Jessica Rabbit look, with a dress like this, it will work as is. For a shorter dress, continue to Step 4.

4. To sew together a high slit, turn the dress inside out, pin the slit together, and begin to stitch, starting at the very top using a running stitch again. Continue sewing until about 1 inch past the length you want it to be, then cut the dress with scissors. If you go the no-sew route, grab some fabric glue and dab between the underside of the pinned down fabric to keep the hem together.

5. Fold under, pin the raw edges down, and stitch a new hem, either by hand (running stitch again) or with a sewing machine using a straight stitch.

From dated to classic red velvet dress. Cannot go wrong with this one.

PURPLE LACE STRAPLESS DRESS

Dressipe

- **Dress**
- **Seam ripper**
- **Scissors**
- **Straight pins**
- **Elastic and fabric markers, if necessary**
- **Sewing machine, or hand needle, and thread (sew option)**
- **Safety pins (no-sew option)**

The satin accents, the sequins, and the train are a hot-mess trifecta. This won't work outside of Halloween or dancing in a Van Halen video.

1. First, use a seam ripper and scissors to carefully remove all unwanted embellishments and fabric. All the purple satin, plus the puffy material, sleeves, and the train had to go, followed by the sequins and the lace on the bodice.

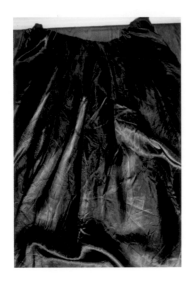

2. Stitch the top of the garment back together to re-create a polished neckline now that the embellishments are gone. Similar to this chapter's Look #1, Red Velvet Dress (p. 63), hand stitch the openings where trim was removed with a running stitch or use a straight stitch on the sewing machine. For the non-sewers, use safety pins to keep the neckline together, pinning them from the inside of the dress.

3. To create new straps for the dress, measure enough elastic to fit from your bust area, over the shoulder, and to your mid-back, preferably in a color that goes with the shade of the dress. (If you don't have matching elastic, use white elastic, and color it with fabric markers in a matching shade.) If you'd rather keep this dress strapless, skip this step and the next one and end here.

4. Take the elastic and pick even spots by the shoulders on each side of the dress where you'll affix new straps, both in the front and back.

Hand stitch the elastic in place with a running stitch a few times back and forth until it's secure when you pull it, or use safety pins to attach the straps.

Now a simplified dress from all that business . . . I think I can open a satin boutique with what I've got leftover . . . SATINICITY, SATINESSENCE, SATINCAKE FACTORY . . . name is still TBD.

look #3

PINK LACE DRESS

Dressipe

- **Dress**
- **Seam ripper**
- **Straight pins**
- **A swatch of lace**
- **Scissors**
- **Sewing machine, or hand needle, and thread (sew option)**
- **Fabric glue (no-sew option)**

Sheer black material and a big ol' bow front and center? No! Keep it simple, sister—KISS—the anagram that was drilled into my head by an old teacher, except I changed the last word to be nice. To add a little pop to this gorgeously simple base, I chose to add pink lace down the front of this dress.

1. Use a seam ripper to remove any unwanted embellishments (like that hideous ribbon and the velvet sleeves).

2. Fold under and pin the raw edges where the sleeves were removed, preparing to stitch them down about a $1/4$ inch.

4. Use a running stitch by hand or a straight stitch on a sewing machine to permanently affix the pink lace to the dress with matching pink thread. For a no-sew option, go with fabric glue to tack down the lace.

With some removing here and some adding there, this dress is classy enough to swig old-fashioneds with Don Draper.

3. Measure a square of pink lace that will fit in the V area between the velvet fabric on the chest. (I used a swatch of lace measuring 8 × 4 inches.) Use scissors to trim the lace so it fits perfectly within the V area. Pin down the lace around the edges onto the top of the fabric to secure.

look #4

m.o.b. dress

Dressipe

- **M.O.B. dress**
- **Seam ripper**
- **Scissors**

I see these Mother of the Bride dresses all the time. They seem to be staple pieces that stick around season after season—beads and shimmer up top and chiffon down below. I'm only going to wear this if I'm walking my child down the aisle with Dorothy Zbornak, Rose Nylund, Blanche Devereaux, and Sophia Petrillo, so until then . . .

1. Use a seam ripper to separate the beaded top from bottom of the skirt.

Just like Bishop (Lance Henriksen) in *Alien*, except I did it way more tenderly.

2. With the beaded top now on its own, use scissors to trim out the zipper. (When trimming, be careful to stay

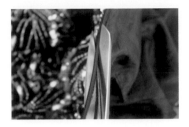

as close to the teeth of the zipper as possible to avoid cutting the actual fabric.)

Super-glitzy jacket in two steps—the beauty of a piece like this is that you can wear it on top of something fance or just pair with a vintage tee and jeans to rock the 'celebrity on my day off' look. From M.O.B. dress to every day . . .

chapter eight

bridesmaid dresses

Marla Singer: I got this dress at a thrift store for one dollar. It's a bridesmaid dress. Someone loved it intensely for one day, then tossed it. Like a Christmas tree. So special. Then, bam, it's on the side of the road. Tinsel still clinging to it. —*Fight Club*

t's like Chuck Palahniuk was secretly speaking to me when he created Marla's character—we're obviously on the same budgety-vintage wavelength. One small note Marla didn't mention: Most bridesmaid dresses don't have anyone intensely loving it for one day—more like being forced to wear it for one day.

I've been in only two weddings and lucked out on the bridesmaid dresses for both. Because of this, I've asked for some help.

This is the true story of unnamed girls, asked to share their stories to find out what happens when bridesmaids stop being polite . . . and start getting real. "The Real World: Bridesmaid Dresses."

"Turquoise strapless sateen mermaid dresses. Dead of winter. Outdoor reception."

"Pepto-Bismol pink strapless dresses that were unflattering on everyone. In photos we looked like we were wrapped in towels, *very* expensive towels."

"Six words: *Gone With the Wind* themed wedding. I felt like Donna Martin at prom."

"I was the maid of honor at my BFF's wedding. She picked out a frightening *Sleeping-Beauty*-meets-*Nutcracker* plum-colored number. And no, she didn't get married at Disneyland."

"I managed to be a bridesmaid in two weddings that both chose celery as the dress color. Celery is meant for a crudités platter, and that's all."

I've found a few not-so-chic b'maid gowns to show you that they can most definitely be worn twice, just maybe not in the same way.

(PS, girlfriends: I promise not to make you wear anything hideous, and if I lose my mind for a moment and ponder a shade of electric green, just pull a Cher from *Moonstruck* and snap me out of it.)

look #1

sequin
CITY

Dressipe

- **Bridesmaid dress**
- **Seam ripper**
- **Chalk, pencil, or a fabric crayon**
- **Ruler (or straightedge object)**
- **Scissors**
- **Fray Check**

Beyond those sleeves is a party dress waiting to happen!

1. Use a seam ripper to carefully remove the straps from the sequined bodice.

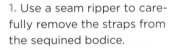

2. Pin down the areas of the sequined body that come to a point in the front and back to make it straight and even, like a tube top. Because of the sequins and tricky nature of sewing them on a machine without breaking needles, hand stitch the four points under with a running stitch.

3. Choose your desired length. For a wedding, long works. For a party dress, it's all about short and sweet. (I decided on a tea length.) If you cut the dress, use chalk to mark your line just because it's easier to rub off and remove without leaving residue since this piece won't have a stiched hem. Use scissors to trim along your line.

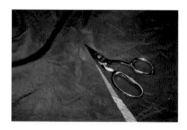

4. It's time to fix your hem. I used Fray Check, a glorious non-sewing trick to keep the raw edges from fraying (it's basically like a liquid seal). Dab it all around the edges of the dress, making sure to coat every edge. This is a great time-saver to get the same hem that you would from stitching and does the trick for those sew-phobics!

5. Let the dress dry for about 30 minutes before wearing.

Let's get the party started!

Fray Check Tip

Fray Check should work like a charm on most fabrics; however, test out a small section before you begin using. A spot on the inside of the garment is ideal to experiment with and to make sure the fabric doesn't discolor.

look #2

medieval times

Dressipe

- **Bridesmaid dress**
- **Seam ripper**
- **Scissors**
- **Iron**
- **Straight pins**
- **Sewing machine, or hand needle, and thread (sew option)**
- **Fray Check (no-sew option)**

Under the layers of chiffon, there's a dress ready to be worn by someone other than Maid Marian (or you in the "great idea" for a wedding that your BFF had). For this piece, it's about removing the gray chiffon.

1. Use a seam ripper to carefully remove the sleeves.

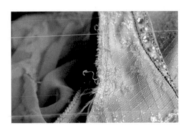

2. Once sleeves are removed, snip off the top layer of the skirt, the gray chiffon. Snip as close to the seam as possible to get the cleanest trim.

bridesmaid dresses ⊕ 77

3. Pick your desired length for the dress (mine is knee length), fan it out on the floor (because you want the entire skirt part laid flat), draw a line across with chalk half an inch below your chosen length (save for the hem) and trim it. Because of the flowy nature of the dress, when you fan it on the ground and trim, make sure you follow the original hem. Unlike dresses that have straight skirts (i.e., red velvet dress on p. 63) where cutting a straight line works, in flowier dresses like these, following the original hem prevents the edges from being longer on the outside than in the center.

sewing, use Fray Check to finish the edges. (Follow steps from this chapter's Look #1 sequined bodice dress, p. 75)

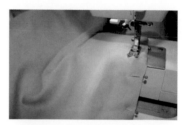

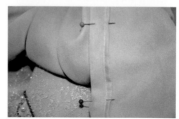

The dress has made a 180 and no longer looks like a costume in *Robin Hood: Prince of Thieves*. However, I welcome the playing of Bryan Adams's "(Everything I Do) I Do It For You" anytime.

4. Fold under and pin the bottom to create a hem (skip to chapter 2: Muumuu Transformations, pp. 13–14, for walk-through) and either sew a running stitch by hand or a straight stitch by machine to finish the edges. To avoid

look #3

BLACK & WHITE LACE

Dressipe

- **Bridesmaid dress**
- **Fabric dye (I went with RIT dye in Purple.)**
- **Salt**
- **Washing machine/dryer**
- **Seam ripper**
- **Straight pins**
- **Sewing machine, or hand needle, and thread (sew option)**
- **Stitch Witchery (no-sew option)**

For a light-colored brides-maid dress to guarantee an-other wear, dyeing is an easy trick.

1. Select your dye color and prep your washing machine for the dye. Select a WHITES or HOT WATER cycle.

2. Add the dye (about half a bottle) and a cup of salt to the running water in the machine.

3. Place the dress under the running water to get it thor-oughly soaked (this assists in smooth dye distribution). Once saturated, add it to the dye bath and let the washing machine complete its cycle.

5. Use a seam ripper to remove any unwanted material or accents. (I took off the fluffy bottom with the lace.)

6. Fold under and pin the rough edges to prepare a hem, and either hand stitch, machine stitch, or use Stitch Witchery (Refer to chapter 12: Look #1 Stitch Witchery for an in-depth how-to on p. 117) to permanently adjust the hem.

New color and a simplified shape make this a hot tamale dress ready for a cocktail party.

4. Post-wash, throw the dress into the dryer. Make sure you run another wash without clothes just to make sure you get out any dye remnants!

(See chapter 13 "I Dye" for more dye tips.)

You're like the maid of dishonor.
—*Bridesmaids*

You make someone a bridesmaid, and they
sh*t all over you.—*Sixteen Candles*

Always a bride, never a bridesmaid!
—*Runaway Bride*

HONORABLE MENTION

This quote has nothing to do with
dresses, but is just as disturbing as
some of the other tell-alls that I
received . . .

"My sister was in a wedding in
which she was told which manufac-
turer of stockings/nylons were
acceptable to wear. Seriously."

chapter nine

costume party

I love celebrations and gatherings, but even more, I love dressing up! From theme parties (*Mad Men* cocktail soirees are the best; I don't enjoy drinking Tom Collinses, but I'll drink them down to the last drop just to stay in character) to themed cooking club dinners and holidays like Halloween (hello homemade Heather Graham in *Boogie Nights,* Uma Thurman in *Pulp Fiction* . . . basically those actresses have to keep working just to give me costumes to re-create because of the kinda-resemblance) to dress-up days at work (I'll wear USC or Jets colors, loud and proud on sports team day). Putting together a proper ensemble to celebrate is a super-fun way to get your craft on.

At the end of the day, there's nothing better than budgeting and avoiding Halloween stores like the plague during this totally fun holiday. You'll save money, you won't go insane because of long lines, and you won't show up to find three other people dressed in the same bagged costume.

Cheap + unique = winning Halloween costume!

look #1

KILL BILL

Dressipe

- **Work space cover (news-papers, shower curtain, or old towel)**
- **Hoodie/pant set (I used a zip-up/yoga pant set from Alternative Apparel.)**
- **Fabric dye (I used RIT dye in Lemon Yellow and Cherry Red.)**
- **Salt**
- **Washing machine/dryer**
- **Straw**
- **Ribbon (I used black gros-grain.)**
- **Scissors**
- **Cardboard boxes or paper shopping bags**
- **Hand needles and black thread (sew option to affix ribbon)**
- **Fabric glue or glue gun, and glue sticks (no-sew option to affix ribbon)**

- **Other Uma accoutre-ments: plastic samurai sword (I borrowed a real one, but it's probably not a good idea toting that puppy around on Hallow-een), fake blood for hands/chest if desired, black sneakers or boots.**

The main component to this costume is the tracksuit. A zipable top and a pair of drawstring pants, which could easily come from your dresser drawers—track pants, yoga pants, sweats—any of these will work great, and un-less they come in yellow al-ready, a lighter shade is ideal to work with because dye is being used to match the top/pants combo and it will best absorb a bold yellow shade.

1. To get started on the Black Mamba ensemble, and the yellow dyeing, begin a HOT WATER wash in the washing machine, adding a cup of salt to the bath and then using an entire bottle or powder pack-age of lemon yellow dye. (I took my Alternative Apparel zip-up and pants and added a bottle of RIT's Yellow dye to get a super bold color.)

2. Soak the hoodie and pants in water (this assists in smooth dye distribution), then add them to the yellow dye bath in the washing machine.

3. Post-wash, toss the pieces into the dryer for a quick spin.

4. Once the hoodie and pants are out of the dryer, affix black ribbon ($\frac{1}{2}$ inch to 1 inch works, but go thicker or thinner depending on preference and what you may already have in your kit) to the arms of the hoodie and the sides of the pant legs. (I used Aleene's Flexible Stretchable Fabric Glue because it's easy to apply and stays affixed as you move.) Insert a piece of cardboard or thick paper into the arms of the hoodie and the legs of the pants to prevent the fabric from sticking to itself while being glued. (Repurpose a shipping box or grocery store bags and cut a strip that fits within the sleeves/pant legs.)

Depending on how much time you've got, you can use a hand stitch or machine stitch (see pp. 5–9), or hot glue the black ribbon, staple the black ribbon . . . any way to get it to stay in place.

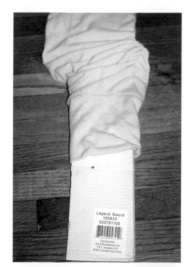

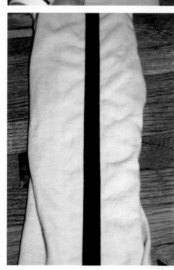

5. Dab glue onto the ribbon and press it securely onto all four lengths. Let the ribbon dry overnight (or at least 2 hours) before removing the cardboard.

6. Add a bit more realness—faux blood—as a final touch. Since you won't need that much dye (1 cup max), microwave a paper cup of water until boiling or boil water in a dye-only pot on the stove (you want to reap at least a cup of dyed water, so fill your pot accordingly). Add a sprinkle of salt and a teaspoon or so of red RIT dye. Add enough to reach your desired shade of crimson.

Before you begin to splatter, make sure you put down something to cover your work space to avoid a fake bloodbath! Take a plastic garbage bag or an old shower curtain and cover your kitchen table or floor. Use a straw to splatter the red dye on the hoodie and pants. (I dipped the straw into my dye, put my thumb on the top as a suction, and drizzled it over the neck and flicked it directly at the hoodie to get different blood patterns. I watch too much *Dexter.*)

To make some darker spots (dried blood), dip the straw directly into the dye bottle and dab away. The dye should dry overnight and come morning, you'll have a suit ready to channel your inner Uma Thurman.

Cue the whistling now. (PS: That whistling tune from *Kill Bill* is "Twisted Nerve" by Bernard Herrmann.)

look #2

LUCILLE BALL

Dressipe

- **Dress (preferably with polka dots)**
- **Seam ripper**
- **Scissors**
- **Straight pins**
- **Sewing machine, or hand needle, and thread (sew option)**
- **Safety pins (no-sew option)**
- **Other Lucy accoutrements: curls, red lipstick, bonbons! (I used Trader Joe's truffles.)**

"Lucy, I'm home!"

To work your inner Lucille Ball, the main component for this ensemble is polka dots! She's the polka-dot queen, so this pattern should be on your radar when trying to find the perfect thrifted dress.

This red-and-white polka-dot dress was just the piece to work for a Lucy look-alike. The red trim around the collar was perfect, but the rest of the upper area felt a bit frumpy.

1. Use a seam ripper to remove the sleeves.

2. If the areas under the arms are still big, you will want to take in the body enough to make it more fitted. Try on the dress, pinch the excess fabric along the side of the torso, and pin the ideal spot for the new seam to sit. Using a straight stitch with a sewing machine or a running stitch by hand, create your new seam, stitch over the pins, and remove them when finished. Trim the excess material, if there is a lot of it, with scissors.

3. Fold under and pin the raw edges around the armhole next and sew them by hand or by sewing machine, or use safety pins to keep them in place.

Now the dress is ready for some bonbons! Fill 'er up!

look #3

marilyn monroe

Dressipe

- **Dress (preferably white with a full skirt)**
- **Seam ripper**
- **Scissors**
- **Straight pins**
- **Sewing machine, or hand needle, and thread (sew option)**
- **Safety pins (no-sew option)**
- **Other Marilyn accoutrements: red lipstick and faux mole (unless you're rocking a real one above the lips), portable fan (if you need wind gusts on the go).**

Mole, red lips, *Some Like it Hot,* Norma Jean, Happy Birthday, white dress . . . "Who is Marilyn Monroe, Alex!"

Marilyn is associated with so many things, but that white dress is downright historical. To find the perfect white dress, the skirt is key—look for something flowy in case a subway grate happens to be underneath your feet. Even though it wasn't a halter, this dress had the potential to become Marilyn-esque.

1. Use a seam ripper to remove the sheer sleeves and cut the neck.

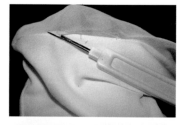

2. In trying to re-create the deep V now that the neck has been removed, begin to tuck the fabric under and pin it in place starting at the shoulders and going all the way down to the bust area to create a similar line to Marilyn's halter. You're looking to make that V-shape, so keep that in mind as you tuck and pin.

3. With the raw edges of the armholes and new neckline pinned under, sew them down. Hand stitching a running stitch or machine stitching a straight stitch using white thread will complete the dress.

4. To make the dress fitted, à la Marilyn, take in the body of the dress as many inches as necessary to achieve complete snugness, or use safety pins to gather the material. (Refer to Look #2: Lucille Ball, pp. 88–89, for a rundown on taking in the dress.)

All you need to complete the look are some platinum curls, a faux mole, and red lips. Well, hello Mr. President!

look #4

alice in wonderland

Dressipe

- **Dress**
- **Seam ripper**
- **Chalk, pencil, or a fabric crayon**
- **Ruler (or straightedge object)**
- **Scissors**
- **Straight pins**
- **White fabric (old shirt, cloth napkins—something for an apron)**
- **Ribbon (I used the leftover sash from the dress, but a blue or white satin or grosgrain works well.)**
- **Sewing machine, or hand needle, and thread (sew option)**
- **Fray Check, tape, Stitch Witchery, or safety pins (no-sew option)**
- **Other Alice accoutrements: headband, stockings/lace socks, Mary Janes, blond wig, and a rabbit.**

I always wanted to be Alice in Wonderland at Disneyland. If I wasn't taller than the maximum height, that might have been my side job while I was going to college! Since it was not, I have to make my own costume to wear on Halloween . . . or on my next trip to Disneyland!

The keys to this piece are the color and the neckline. In thrifting, keep your eyes peeled for both of these elements, and if the color is off, look for something in white with the perfect neckline and dye it powder blue. (Check RIT's color formula guide to find the perfect match at ritdye.com.)

1. When flea marketing or garage saleing, give the garment a once-over, looking for any tears or defects in the fabric. Sometimes too great of a tear isn't worth purchasing, but a lot of the time you can make it work. (Here, the white cuffs on the sleeves were torn, so I removed them on both sides.) Use scissors to cut off problem areas like sleeves and frayed edges.

2. Use a seam ripper to remove any unwanted elements. (Here the blue sashes stitched at the waist were taken off to be used in Step 6.) Preserve the excess trimmings, embellishments, and fabric, as they can be repurposed elsewhere in the dress or in other pieces in the future. (see chapter 15: Leftovers, for other uses for excess fabric)

3. Decide how long or short you want the dress to be. Alice's dress generally sits just above the knee. Measure your length and draw a line across the fabric, leaving 1 inch of excess material to save for the hem.

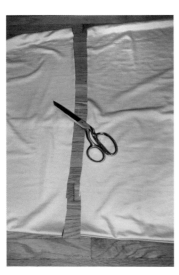

4. Pin down the raw edges of the sleeves and the bottom of the dress and sew new seams. Stitch a running seam by hand, sew a straight stitch with a sewing machine, or go the tape or Fray Check route. (Go to chapter 2: Muumuu Transformations, p. 11; to read steps in creating a seam or using tape, p. 18; and for using Fray Check, see p. 76.)

5. It's not Alice if it doesn't have an apron. Measure a rectangle out of fabric (a cloth napkin, an old pillow—I used an old white blouse). It should go lengthwise from your waist to mid-thigh area, and the width should span the front of your legs.

6. Once the white material has been cut, sew a seam around the edges and use ribbon (white or blue works well) or a sash that is long enough to go around your waist with an additional foot for tying a bow. (In my case, I used the sashes that were removed from the dress in Step 1). Stitch, safety pin, glue, or use Stitch Witchery to the top of the white fabric. Make sure to line up the center of the cut ribbon with the center of the apron material.

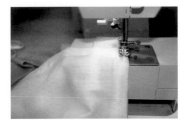

With some lace socks, patent heels, a short blond wig, and a brass rabbit, my Alice was complete—the wig gave it an edgier David Lynch kind of vibe that I was totally down with. I mean we do share the same last name . . .

PRETTY IN PINK

Dressipe

- **Lace and polka-dot dress options**
- **Scissors**
- **Straight pins**
- **Sewing machine, or hand needle, and thread (sew option)**
- **Glue gun and glue sticks, or safety pins (no-sew option)**
- **Other Andie accoutrements: prom purse, prom date.**

Obviously, I'm a total Andie Walsh. I shopped my way through T.J.Maxx as a kid and worked at an aromatherapy store, which was the '90s equivalent to Trax, except for scents instead of sounds. Like Andie, I was going to rock something handmade for my prom, so I made a purse straight out of the DIY pages of *Sassy* (I heart Jane Pratt). I didn't have as much time in high school—always trying to bulk up the résumé for college—otherwise an entire dress could have been crafted. So, now's my time. I'm doing my version of *Pretty in Pink*. . . . Isn't she?

The key to this dress was the pink and white polka-dot fabric and the lace for the top. Two dresses were found that fit the bill—one to use for the lace neckline and the other to use for the body.

1. Use scissors to carefully remove the lace top from the magenta dress. Place the lace over the top of the polka-dot dress and match shoulders. Use scissors to trim the lace so that it matches and fits the shape of the polka-dot dress at the top, as this is where it will be sewn in place.

2. Use scissors to remove the neck of the polka-dot dress. (I removed the area right below the collarbone in front and midway down the back of the dress.) Molly Ringwald left the shoulders draping, so use a seam ripper to separate the seams between the sleeves and the body before trimming.

3. Pin the lace to the top of the polka-dot dress (right sides facing each other) around the edges of the lace fabric and do the same on the back.

4. Once the lace is pinned, stitch together the lace and polka-dot dress. Use a running stitch by hand or a straight stitch by machine on a 2.5 stitch setting since the lace is delicate. Safety pins totally do the trick as well.

Andie had her dress after some cutting and sewing and you can too! You want to get the essence of the DIY nature, so be creative and have an open mind.

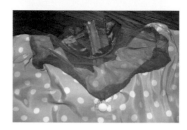

Now all I need is my personal Duckie because I am definitely not getting stood up by Blane.

chapter 10

TRANSITION PIECES

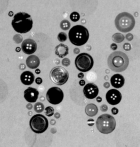hen I was a kid and everyone wanted to be a veterinarian or a marine biologist, I wanted to be a lawyer (totally courtesy of *L.A. Law* and Victor Sifuentes because Jimmy Smits was that good) but ended up going to journalism school in college instead. I interned my face off because I was in constant fear of not getting a job once I graduated, then got work in a completely different field, and now I'm sewing. Moral of the story, like Exposé sang in their 1988 jam, "Seasons Change."

That doesn't just go for the weather . . .

- Brussels sprouts always tasted bitter and unpleasant to me until I tried the holy grail of sprouts in Los Angeles, made with bacon. Life-changing sprouts, I tell ya!
- The dream of a perm as a teen was kicked to the curb by my mom who brilliantly knew it was a bad idea, even though all my friends had them. Looking back, it was the one dream I'd have her crush over and over again.

Over time we change. I was petrified before I turned thirty and then had an epiphany moment where I realized that there was nothing to be done about it. I could either embrace the change or wallow in it. I went the embracing route and have never felt better.

Same thing goes with clothes: styles change, tastes change, sizes change. These are things that can benefit from a little overhaul. Perms don't go away. That's why they're called permanents. Clothes don't have that title and there is always wiggle room. Time to wiggle.

look #1

corporate pants turned shorts

Dressipe

- **Dress pants**
- **Chalk, pencil, or a fabric crayon**
- **Ruler (or straightedge object)**
- **Scissors**
- **Straight pins**
- **Sewing machine, or hand needle, and thread, if desired**

Just because you got your dream job in graphic design or event planning doesn't mean you need to toss those dress pants you used to wear every day.

Those trousers are still going to work, but they're going to look much different in three snips, I mean steps, I mean snips.

1. Use scissors to trim each pant leg an inch below knee-level. Mark a line with a ruler if it's easier.

2. Pin raw edges under and hand stitch a running stitch or machine sew a straight stitch around for a hem. If you don't want to sew, just skip to Step 3.

3. Fold and roll up the edges a few times and you've got shorts in a jiffy.

Pair with tights, fun shoes, and a casual top and your new artistic work environment ensemble is complete. "Workin' 9 to 5, what a way to make a livin'."

look #2

JUNGLE TOP TURNED VEST

Dressipe

- **Sweater top**
- **Seam ripper**
- **Scissors**
- **Straight pins**
- **Sewing machine, or hand needle, and thread (sew option)**
- **Fray Check and safety pins (no-sew option)**

Who else attended a slew of theme parties in college? Austin Powers Shagalicious (it was 1999!), check. Mafia theme, check. Jungle party, check. I loved heading downtown to the garment district to find cheap pieces for these shindigs, but can they ever work again . . . especially once you've graduated and aren't dressing up on a weekly basis? Yeah, baby!

Take this sweater from the jungle party ensemble. Paired with a leopard skirt and stilettos, I was literally Jocelyn Wildenstein, Queen of the Jungle, sans all that plastic

surgery. This outfit won't see the light of day again in its current incarnation, but it will soon be jungle party no more and can come with you post-graduation.

1. Use a seam ripper to remove bits of unwanted fabric (like this black ribbed collar) and, if desired, the sleeves.

2. If, like mine, your top has buttons going all the way up to the neck or another un-wanted front closure, you can repurpose it as a vest. Fold under the left and right sides at the top of the front at a 30-degree angle and pin. **I used the buttons as a guide of how low to go. The V goes down to the third button from the top.**

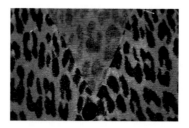

3. Pin down the rough edges of the neckline where the collar was removed, and the sleeves if they were taken off as well. Use a straight stitch if sewing by machine or a running stitch if sewing by hand and stitch down (over the pins) the top, collar, and sleeves. Use Fray Check for the sleeves, and safety pins to keep the neck down for a no-sew option.

The long-sleeved, terrycloth, collared shirt now rocks as a vest that can be worn anywhere, leaving no remnants of jungle party lingering behind. Jungle juice never tasted that good anyway.

QUICK TRICK!

For those sleeves that don't stay rolled up—Take a rubber band or hair elastic, move it over your triceps, and roll the sleeves around the band. Your sleeves will stay in place, and you'll have an extra elastic if you want to make pigtails.

chapter eleven

quick no-sew
fixes in minutes.
yes, minutes

I was a product of the '80s, for sure. I loved Mr. T Cereal **"I Pity the Fool!,"** loved wearing big hanging earrings **(my earlobes have stretched thanks to those heavy danglers),** and loved watching TV. I don't know if I was subconsciously inspired, but *MacGyver* was one show that I was obsessed with. I mean, Richard Dean Anderson stopped bombs with gum wrappers, a Swiss Army knife, and panty hose on the regular. That's pretty badass, and he did it with a full-on mullet and brown leather bomber.

I like to think of myself as a fashion MacGyver of sorts. I didn't fare well in Chemistry **(I loved melting glass into rings with the Bunsen burner but after that "Chem 101" stage, I was out),** but coming up with quick tricks to avoid mini fashion disasters on the fly? Bring it.

I'm pretty confident that in a time crunch I'd be able to make it work with whatever I have on me. These pieces came to fruition after some quick thinking. Grab those safety pins because it's time to go from blerg to beautiful!

look #1

CINCH AND PINCH—

Dressipe

- **Dress with thick straps/ wide V-neck collar**
- **Safety pins**

This is one of my favorite tricks as it changes the entire look of a dress in just one step, giving a softer and more feminine look. And it takes less than a minute.

This trick works for dresses that have a V-neck, are boxy topped, or are wrap styled—ones with thicker straps in general. For dresses that may be bigger up top, this also works because it tightens the bust area without having to sew a lick.

1. Grab one strap slightly below the collarbone with your thumb and index finger and pinch it together.

2. Take a safety pin, push it through the cinched fabric, and fasten it closed.

3. Repeat the above step on the other side.

Two of my favorite words to live by, cinch and pinch.

OTHER CINCHING TOOLS

If a safety pin is out of reach, feel free to substitute with ribbon, string, or even a pipe cleaner.

look #2

Gross To Gorg—Fabric Removal

Dressipe

- **Dress with removable items (i.e., patches, collar, or appliqués)**
- **Seam ripper**

Like I mentioned earlier, when out and about on shopping trips, keeping your eyes peeled for fabric that strikes you is key. Don't be turned off by extra add-ons like dangling beads or taxicab patches (yes, that one exists!) that may date the piece or make it less intriguing. You can usually fix it.

That's exactly the case for this dress. It's got a great late '60s/early '70s Carol Brady feel, but that white collar is a little much.

1. Use a seam ripper to remove the stitches and detach the collar from the dress.

One step and the collar is removed. Easy peasy.

chapter twelve

MY BFF, THE IRON

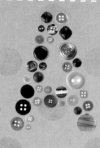n iron is a beautiful thing. Not only does it take wrinkles out of shirts, it can be used to straighten hair in time of need and can even make a delicious sandwich in a stoveless dorm room if you're craving something melty. It's really a multifunctional tool and I love mine for reasons that go beyond the above.

Reason 1: For iron-ons.
Reason 2: For Stitch Witchery.

I'm pretty much obsessed with personalization, from initialed stationery to charm bracelets to my old monogrammed L.L.Bean backpack from elementary school. Maybe it's my fondness for typography or just my love of detail, but I was the one hanging out at the engraving kiosk at the mall seeing what people were getting inscripted on those key chains during the holidays. Since I don't have a fancy engraving machine, I've got to work with what I've got, and what I've got is an iron and some iron-ons. Personalizing onesies for friends' new babies—obsessed. Adding letters to a top to make an awesome costume—obsessed. **(I still wear the "Seniors" tank, à la *Dazed and Confused*, that I made for a theme party years ago).** Adding numbers to the back of a shirt to root for my favorite Yankees' player—obsessed. Thanks to my iron, just call me an at-home Things Remembered.

Stitch Witchery is kind of like my sewing version of CliffsNotes. OK, I confess . . . I was totally a CliffsNotes'er back in high school. I'd read the book **(ahem, *Les Misérables*, sophomore year),** but use those yellow-and-black-striped pamphlets as my totable tutor. Mini shortcuts to help understand and refresh the memory when I'd pass out midway through reading a chapter the night before. That's how I see Stitch Witchery. It's a little shortcut that just helps me get to that end point faster. No sewing and just ironing on of fusible tape to secure my hem? Brilliant, and not cheating at all.

So, that's how I feel about my iron. If my iron could share a "Best Friends" necklace with me without burning the necklace **(metal around hot metal—no bueno)** it would definitely have the "Be Fri" half.

look #1

STITCH WITCHERY

Dressipe

- **Dress/long skirt**
- **Chalk, pencil, or a fabric crayon**
- **Ruler (or straightedge object)**
- **Scissors**
- **Iron**
- **Cloth**
- **Straight pins**
- **Stitch Witchery**

Stitch Witchery is a splendid thing. It's fusible tape that makes fabric stick together when put between two pieces and ironed. For those without sewing machines it's brilliant and a killer quick fix to get the same hem you would if you were using a machine.

For any piece going from long to short, here's how you do it.

1. Pick a length that you'd like your dress to be, measure a line with a marking utensil, remembering to leave an extra inch for the hem, and cut with scissors.

2. Fold under the raw edges, and iron the edges down.

3. Get out the roll of Stitch Witchery and cut a 5-inch section. I like to trim pieces of SW and add it as I go around the hem with an iron on the ironing board.

4. Place the Stitch Witchery between the two undersides (dull sides) of the fabric. Use a damp cloth, per SW instructions, to dab the fabric where the Stitch Witchery was added. The dampness mixed with the heat of the iron will fuse the SW in place.

5. Put the iron on the wool setting, and begin to press down on top of the cloth and fabric and Stitch Witchery for 10 or so seconds. Make sure you're pressing down and dabbing instead of gliding across. Do this on both sides of the fabric and let the garment cool (30 seconds or so) before moving on.

6. Trim another piece of Stitch Witchery and repeat the above step until you make your way around the entire dress and the fabric is bonded with the SW.

Insta-hem without a lick of sewing.

look #2

iron-on
Lettering

Dressipe

- **Jersey/T-shirt/baby onesie**
- **Iron-on lettering (I used Dritz 1^1/$_2$-inch Soft Flock Iron-On Letters.)** Tip: The fuzzy/velvety iron-on letters tend to work better for me
- **Scissors**
- **Iron**

My Rowenta travel iron comes with me everywhere—for on-the-go pressing to on-the-go personalizing. Nothing's better than a homemade onesie for a pal's baby, or a jersey emblazoned with your favorite team that didn't cost a pretty penny on NFL.com.

Depending on the color of the garment, pick a contrasting shade of iron-on lettering to adhere. White on white or red on red just doesn't work, friends.

Using white lettering and an old green pinnie snagged from my brother's closet **(thanks, Dane!),** I'm making a personalized JETS jersey because I'm from NY and they're my hometown football team.

1. Use scissors to cut out your selected letters from the transfer sheet of A, B, Cs.

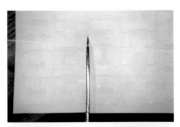

2. Once cut, space out the letters adhesive side down (paper side up) and place them in your desired spot.

3. Set your iron to a dry/cotton setting—one without steam—and wait until it is hot. The letters need a hot setting to affix properly. Press the letters in place, holding the iron over each letter for about 30 seconds, or the specified length of time on the instructions that came with the lettering. Once each letter has been individually ironed, iron them all again, going back and forth in figure 8s for another 15 seconds.

4. When finished ironing, the paper backing will be hot, so watch your fingers and test each letter by pulling at the corners to see if they have adhered before peeling off. If they haven't fully stuck, go over the letters again with the iron, then peel off the paper backing when ready.

Now the pinnie is ready to be worn to root for my team! J-E-T-S, JETS, JETS, JETS!

This is also a great way to personalize a onesie for your favorite little dude or gal.

look #3

iron-on transfer paper

Dressipe

- **T-shirt/tank top**
- **Printer transfer paper (I used Tulip Photo Transfer Paper.)**
- **Printer**
- **Scissors (if trimming around the image is needed)**
- **Iron**

Since I deemed myself the fashion MacGyver, I just had to pay homage to my creative television serial icon, Robert Dean Anderson (in his leather bomber and mullet glory) with an iron-on T-shirt.

1. Using iron-on transfer paper, and following the package directions, pick an image (I found an image of MacGyver) on your computer, and print it onto the transfer paper using a basic color printer. My printer is no-frills and it worked great.

2. Once you've printed your image, place the sheet directly onto the shirt. With an iron (on a dry setting), press on top of the paper for about 30 seconds, going over each spot of the transfer until the heat fuses the paper to the fabric.

3. Let cool for at least 2 minutes before peeling off the paper backing.

The paper backing will be hot so watch your fingers when removing.

Personalized iron-on transfer in minutes? That's right! I grabbed my tools and took to the streets, MacGyver-style.

SEWING PLAYLIST

Sewing has always been my fun time, so I like to jam when I'm winding that bobbin. Plus, the right music makes projects go by faster. From a mix of old-school faves from my teen years to songs that allow me to have a private karaoke sesh from the comfort of my home, here's what I listen to . . .

- Aloe Blacc—"I Need A Dollar" (that's right!)
- Black Kids—"I'm Not Gonna Teach Your Boyfriend How to Dance With You" (I totally air drum to this when I'm spinning thread onto my bobbin!)
- David Bowie—"Rebel Rebel" (Bowie makes everything better)
- Elton John—"Benny and the Jets" (not just because the Jets are my favorite team . . . I get to scream Benny over and over)
- Justin Timberlake—"Like I Love You" ("Here baby, hold my jacket," is obviously my favorite line)
- Loverboy—"Working for the Weekend" (this just gets me revved up)
- MGMT—"Electric Feel" (my groovy, shoulders moving, sometimes hand-in-the-air song that just always makes me happy)
- Michael Jackson—"Off the Wall" (my all-time favorite MJ jam)
- Montell Jordan—"This Is How We Do It" (basically anything from the *Save the Last Dance* soundtrack is game)
- Phoenix—"Too Young" (mmm, the French band of my dreams, *J'adore.*)
- Prince—"Raspberry Beret" (I like Prince and I like hats)
- Skee-Lo—"I Wish" (a song I belt out like it's my job each time it's on)
- The Roots—"The Seed" (nothing but straight groovin' when it comes to the Roots)

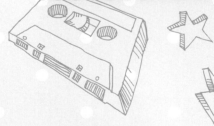

chapter thirteen

I DYe!

I took the immortal words of Rachel Zoe and made them my own: I dye! I heart dye. I loved tie-dyeing shirts in elementary school, and the obsession has stayed with me. I think I just liked seeing anything change color, be it a few drops of green food coloring into Betty Crocker vanilla frosting to turn a cupcake mint, or even those Hypercolor T-shirts that changed color with body heat in 1991. People are super intimidated when it comes to dyeing, but I'm here to show you it's as easy as 1, 2, 3!

You can save a stained **(darn, those wine spills)**, discolored **(blerg, yellowed arms)**, or too sheer **(hello, nipple slip)** piece by giving it a brand-new shade! Pieces that are 100 percent cotton will dye most similar to the shade that's chosen, however, go wild picking and choosing your fabrics. Different fibers will grab on to the dye differently, which is all part of the fun of dyeing.

notes on dyeing

- Fabric dye
- Plastic/rubber gloves
- Salt or vinegar
- Dye pot (solely used for dyeing) or washing machine
- Some sort of workplace cover—newspaper, paint tarp, old shower curtain, etc.
- Plastic squirt bottles, eyedroppers, straws (for a Jackson Pollock effect)
- Rubber bands
- Old pair of scissors to cut rubber bands after dyeing

dye and fabric

What fabrics work best when it comes down to soaking in some color??

SOAK IT UP

- Fabric all-stars include: 100 percent cotton, silk, wool, nylon, rayon, and ramie.
- Non-fabric all-stars include: wood, wicker, paper, feathers, and cork.

ABSORPTION-PHOBIC

- 100 percent polyester, acrylic, acetate, spandex, fiberglass, fabric with metallic fibers.

how much dye to use?

For one pound or three yards of clothing/fabric, use half a bottle of liquid dye or one package of powder dye.

My trick: When I use the washing machine to dye, I adjust the load size to the smallest setting and add a full bottle of dye just to make sure the color is bold enough.

making pieces richer

When dyeing dark or bright colors, you should double the amount of dye used to make the final product richer. Darker shades include navy, black, dark green, brown, purple, and wine.

Salt and vinegar act as agents to make colors bolder and more intense—they're not just the best variety of Lays chips anymore! Keep in mind that salt works better with cottons, rayons, ramies, and linens, while white vinegar works for nylons, silks, and woolens. Dissolve one cup of salt or one cup of white vinegar in your dye bath before you add your garment to soak up the rainbow!

how to clean/launder

Post-dye, hand wash in warm water with a light detergent like Woolite, then with cold water until the dye runs clear. You can add the piece to washes with like colors afterward, but to be on the safe side, your best bet is to hand wash the first few times to prevent bleeding onto other pieces. This will also make the colors last longer. Grab a little Woolite, fill up a sink with cold water, and soak away using the directions on the bottle. Boom.

For any tie-dyed garments with a bunch of white areas, it's smartest to rinse them with cold water the first few times after they've been dyed just to make sure the dye doesn't run—we don't want the newly bull's-eyed designed T-shirt to turn completely navy.

Another safe bet—if you've dyed using the washing machine, make sure to run a HOT WATER wash afterward with a bit of detergent and a cup or two of bleach in the empty machine just to clean out any remaining dye.

There are a few different routes to take to get on the color-changing bandwagon.

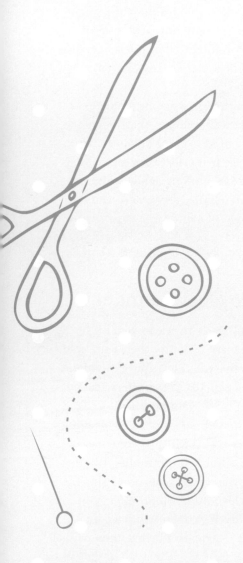

look #1

washing
machine
method

Dressipe

- **Dress/top**
- **Fabric dye (I used RIT dye in Wine.)**
- **Salt or vinegar**
- **Washing machine/dryer**

1. Select your dye color. If you're trying to cover up a spot, go with a shade that's darker than the blemish. (This dress has black markings near the shoulder so I chose RIT dye in Wine as my shade to cover them up.)

2. Prep your washing machine for the dye. Select a WHITES or HOT WATER cycle on the machine.

3. Add about a ¹/₂ bottle of dye and 1 cup salt to the running water in the machine. (For 1 pound of fabric (equiv-

alent to approximately 3 yards), a ¹/₂ bottle (8 oz) of liquid dye, or a full package (1¹/₈ oz.) of powder dye is used) Adding salt or vinegar makes the color really pop.

I'll go with about a 1/2 cup of salt for one cotton piece in the washing machine, but feel free to add more/less depending on how much you've got in your cupboard and how many pieces you're dyeing.

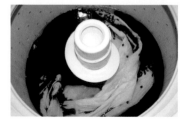

5. Per the dyeing notes on pp. 127–128, after using a washing machine to dye, you want to make sure to clean it out so there are no dye remnants left over. Just run a wash to follow, sans clothes, to make sure it's all cleaned out—add some detergent, some bleach, and let it run like normal, to be on the safe side. It would be a bummer if dye dominated the next wash of your delicate whites, turning them into delicate reds.

If you're dyeing a large dress or multiple pieces, it's ideal to add the dye along with the salt or vinegar to the bath first, before putting in the garment. However, I've added dye after putting just a single piece or two in and it still worked and dyed fine. The one key factor that is a necessity is to make sure that the garment is wet before it touches the colored water. Why must the piece be Toad the Wet Sprocket you ask? This is to prevent splotching and an uneven dye job.

4. The dye and the garment will happily swish together in the washing machine for a half hour or so, then on to the dryer!

I just love that magical moment when you open the lid and there's a whole new shirt! The garment went in white and came out looking like a bottle of Bordeaux. Fitting, as the shade was called Wine. From boring and spotted to fabulous and fun!

look #2

STOVE-TOP METHOD

Dressipe

- **Garment (I used a sheer white blouse.)**
- **Fabric dye (I used RIT dye in Petal Pink with a teaspoon of Sunshine Orange.)**
- **Salt**
- **Dye pot for the stove**
- **Plastic or rubber gloves**
- **Tongs**
- **Sink (to rinse out dye)**

Stove-top dyeing works best with smaller pieces like slips, tanks, and camis. Plus, you can cook dinner at the same time, and I'm all about multi-tasking!

Little FYI—with this method, especially, make sure that you're using plastic or rubber gloves to keep your hands clean.

1. Select a large (about 6 quarts) pot. Fill pot about $^3/_4$ full with water and bring to a boil. Preferably one that won't be used down the road to cook some rigatoni. Keep one pot designated as your "dye pot" that will only be used for dyeing.

2. Turn off the flame and add the dye to the bath.

For up to 1 pound of fabric, use about a $^1/_2$ bottle of liquid dye. If you're using actual measuring cups to gauge, make sure they're solely being used for dye and keep them in your dye kit along with your pot!

3. Add salt to the water. The addition of salt will just enhance the dye color, so don't be stingy. For a 6-quart pot, I use about a ¼ cup of salt, but there is no right or wrong here. Go salt crazy if so inclined!

4. Take the garment and begin soaking it under running water.

5. Once it's fully saturated, place the garment into the dye bath.

The darker the desired color, the longer you should keep the piece in the pot. If I'm going for something super-rich, I let the piece sit overnight. For this, I wanted a bold melon color, so I let the piece soak for a few hours.

6. After keeping the piece in for as long/as little as you fancy, take out the garment, wearing gloves to avoid discoloration of the hands. Be careful and use tongs if the water has not cooled down sufficiently. Wash it out with warm water and Woolite, followed by cold water until the water from the garment runs clear.

7. Ring it out and let it dry.

Nearly see-through no more!

look #3

natural dyes

Dressipe

- **Garment (I used a silk blouse.)**
- **Natural fabric dye (I used Tetley tea.)**
- **Dye pot for the stove**
- **Plastic or rubber gloves**
- **Tongs**
- **Sink (to rinse out dye)**

It's great to have natural dye options, especially ones that come directly from your pantry or cupboards! We're going to use a little bit of tea to dye this vintage silk blouse.

1. Select your tea.

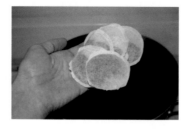

2. Fill up a 6-quart pot about ³/₄ of the way with water and set it to boil. Once the water bubbles, add your tea bags. The amount of tea you use will depend on how dark and saturated (Starbucks espresso) or light (Dunkin' Donuts vanilla latte) you want your piece to be. Let the tea bags steep in the water for a few minutes.

3. Stir the tea bags in the pot. Just like sipping a cup of English breakfast tea, the more times you lift your tea bag, the darker the water becomes.

4. Turn off the stove, remove the tea bags using a spoon, tongs, or ladle—whatever is easy and within reach in the kitch.

5. Soak the garment under running water.

6. Let your piece soak in the dye bath for as long or as short as you'd like, depending on color, until it has turned a shade to your liking. Remove it from the bath carefully, wearing rubber gloves and using tongs.

7. Next, run warm water with Woolite over the garment, then cold water until the water from the garment runs clear to remove any excess dye.

8. It's dry time!

Now you've got a supercute top with an all-natural antique-y finish!

OTHER NATURAL DYES

Other options include coffee, fruits (beets and berries), veggies (carrots and onion skins), spices (curry and tumeric), and even Kool-Aid!

look #4

TIE-DYE TIME!

Dressipe

- **Garment (I used a cotton dress and T-shirt for the spiral style and a pillow-case for the accordion style.)**
- **Fabric dye (I used RIT dyes in multiple shades.)**
  - **spiral style—Teal, Aquamarine, Evening Blue, Royal Blue**
  - **accordion style—Petal Pink, Fuchsia**
- **Salt**
- **Plastic bottles**
- **Plastic or rubber gloves**
- **Rubber bands**
- **Dye work space cover (newspapers, plastic garbage bags, or shower curtain)**

With tie-dyeing, make sure you start with wet garments, just as you would with regular dyeing. Two of my fave designs are the spiral and accordion styles.

spiral style

1. Choose your shades of dye and, wearing gloves, add them to plastic bottles followed by warm water. (I put a tablespoon of dye in each bottle, filled a watering can with water, and added enough to fill each bottle to the top.)

2. To get a spiral, pinwheel look, start with your wet garment laid out flat.

3. Pinch the center of the garment and start twisting. It begins to look like a pre-cooked cinnamon bun when you get closer to the end. (Mmmm . . . Cinnabon.)

4. Once the piece has been twisted to completion, begin placing rubber bands around it to look like spokes on a bicycle. Keep adding to your heart's desire.

5. Begin adding dye to your garment. (Feel free to cover the piece entirely with dye or leave some areas white—the dye will naturally disperse within the garment because it's wet.)

6. After dye has been added, let the garment sit (overnight is best) to absorb as much of the colors as possible.

7. Use scissors to remove the rubber bands and the new piece is fully dyed!

8. Post-dye, wash in warm water with Woolite, then cold water until the water from the garment runs clear.

DIY dye is complete!

accordion style

1. Choose your shades of dye and add them to the water-dropper bottles. I added around two teaspoons of dye to each plastic bottle, then filled them to the top with warm water.

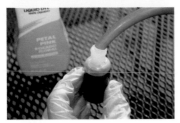

2. To get a an accordion pattern of lines, start with your wet garment laid out.

3. Begin folding and gathering material from the bottom of the piece upward like an accordion. I chose to make my folds horizontal and about 1 inch in width. Have fun with this, because there is no wrong way to do it; create a larger/smaller width and begin with vertical folds if desired. Continue folding until all the material has been gathered.

4. Begin adding rubber bands to the folded garment. I placed them about an inch apart, but place them closer or farther away depending on how much color you want.

5. Once all the bands are at-tached, begin to add dye to the garment. I used two shades of pink and placed them at every other section. Make sure to apply dye to both sides of the material.

6. After the dye has been added, let the garment mari-nate in all the glorious dye. I left mine sitting overnight to absorb as much of the colors as possible.

7. Use scissors to remove rubber bands, and the new piece is complete!

8. Post-dye, wash in warm water with Woolite, then cold water until the water from the garment runs clear.

If only playing an accordion was this easy . . .

chapter fourteen
sentimental

'm a holder-onto-er. I tend to hold on to things for a bit instead of getting rid of them; things attached to memories or things that remind me of other things.

Still holding on to:

- An autograph book from the last day of fourth grade—I missed it due to chicken pox, but my mom went in to get everyone to sign it for me so I wouldn't feel as crappy or itchy.
- A gigantor, red, square **(not the actual Red Square)** candle smelling of cinnamon that an ex-boyfriend gave me.
- Collection of Smurf figurines.
- Leopard-print/sequined unitard costume from a dance recital choreographed to Janet Jackson's "Black Cat."
- Way too many sorority T-shirts from college **(yeah, I was in a sorority . . .)**
- A wedding dress left over from a friend's sketch show.
- A signed cocktail napkin from Brian Dennehy when he ate at a local restaurant on Long Island where we were also dining.
- Garbage Pail Kids cards. **(Babbling Brooke with PB&J covering her face was my fave!)**

In the interim between writing that out and re-reading it, I tossed that candle.

For things on the clothing front that I really don't need but have had difficulty tossing, I've come up with a few tricks to retain them without actually holding on to the whole kit and caboodle.

P.S.: Remember Caboodles? They housed my scrunchies and small bottle of Electric Youth perfume. Le sigh.

look #1

WEDDING DRESS GARTER

Dressipe

- **Wedding dress/lace remnants**
- **Tape measure**
- **Ribbon (I used blue grosgrain.)**
- **Elastic**
- **Scissors**
- **Straight pins**
- **Sewing machine, or hand needle, and thread**
- **Embellishments—optional (vintage charms, pins, or rosettes)**

With that wedding dress . . . even though it's not my mom's or grandmother's, it was somebody's and I'm going to give it a second life by using the fabric and lace to make a garter for someone else's big day. This is a quick and rather easy creation that will give the new bride her something borrowed (and something blue if you add gems or ribbon detail) in that shade. My mom's dress doesn't fit me, so guess what I'm going to do with hers when I get married down the road . . .

1. Use a tape measure and scissors to cut a length of lace and ribbon double the circumference of your thigh.

2. Place pins to secure ribbon to lace and sew the ribbon to the center of the lace, stitching each edge, leaving both ends open, either by hand (running stitch) or using a machine (straight stitch). I matched the blue grosgrain ribbon with blue thread, but if you prefer, you can choose

contrasting colors, since the stitches will be seen.

3. Take elastic (make sure the width is smaller than the ribbon, i.e., if the ribbon is $^3/_4$ inch, then the elastic should be $^2/_3$ inch, or if the ribbon is 1 inch, then the elastic can be $^3/_4$ inch, etc.) and clip a safety pin to one side.

4. Weave the elastic through the center of the ribbon using the safety pin as the guide and pin down each end of the elastic to each end of the ribbon.

5. Stitch the ends of the elastic together, then take the ribbon edges and fold one into the other one and stitch the ends together, tucking the raw edges in.

The garter is wedding-toss ready! You might want to make an extra one for the bride to hold on to . . .

personalize that garter even more

Add a pretty rosette, a vintage earring, or any embellishment to give it an even more personal touch.

look #2

sachet

Dressipe

- **Wedding dress/lace remnants**
- **Round or square pattern to trace (tiles, a coaster, a mug, or the bottom of a vase)**
- **Marking utensil (Sharpie or chalk)**
- **Scissors**
- **Straight pins**
- **Thread**
- **Sewing machine, or hand needle, and thread (sew option)**
- **Fabric glue or glue gun and glue sticks (no-sew option)**
- **Potpourri or rice, with essential oils to fill the sachet**

For those who want something even easier, craft a little sachet and fill it with lavender to hang in your closet or put in dresser drawers.

1. Trace a coaster, bathroom tile, or the bottom of a vase to get a square shape for this.

2. Trim out two squares of the lace remnants from the dress.

3. With the underside of the lace facing out, sew 3 edges of two pieces of lace together. Sew only $1/2$ of the fourth edge, then turn the lace bits inside out. For a no-sew option follow the same step with fabric glue or a glue gun and let dry before turning the lace bits inside out.

4. Fill lace with potpourri, or rice, and some drops of essential oil. Make sure what you fill it with is big enough not to slip through the holes in the lace.

5. Hand stitch or glue the last ½ inch together and the sachet is complete.

The possibilities are endless, because that sachet could also be a beanbag for a classy game of Cornhole. Perhaps even an activity at the wedding reception for the kids . . . or the groomsmen.

Another way to preserve that wedding dress is to cut a swatch, put it in a window box, and hang it on the wall. Romantic-feeling art with sentimental value.

chapter fifteen

LEFTOVERS

Cue summer of 1993. I'm twelve, jamming out to Billy Joel's "River of Dreams"—I was on Long Island, in my dad's Jeep Cherokee, spending much of my vacation at the movies—I saw *Jurassic Park* three times because I was obsessed with the soundtrack and dreamed of being a kid actor in a movie directed by Spielberg and snuck into *The Firm* because I read the book and couldn't wait to see the movie.

I closed the pre-freshman-year vacay with a week at camp in the Catskills with my cousin Erin. And not just any camp—environmental camp. We went fly-fishing, mud mucking **(aka, playing in the mud)**, made crafts with recycled glass, and looked at the stars from the brush. Some kids got their shooter's license. Other kids **(me included)** got slugs in their gear while camping off-site in the rain, while aforementioned campees were getting their shoot on.

One big issue at mealtime has subconsciously stuck with me ever since. There was one big rule at this camp—no waste, period. If it's on your plate, you eat it and if you can't eat it **(or barter or trade it)**, it'll be saved for you until the next mealtime. Usually I'm down to grub; however, when the strawberry short-cake tastes like soap **(I learned the importance of accurately measuring baking powder!)**, and you're forced to chew and swallow, it's hard not to be a little traumatized. The final night's BBQ even had a camper digging a hole under the wooden bench with a fork to bury an uncooked drumstick! The moral of the story is waste not, want not, unless the mandate is unsubstantiated with bogus chow. Now if only I worked my mock trial skills at camp that summer . . .

Because it's hard for me to toss the excess fabric, buttons, and trim from my pieces, I've come up with a few fun **(and easy)** projects that'll use every last bit of them. I promise that I won't force you, though . . .

look #1

SHOe Bags

Dressipe

- **Excess fabric (pieces of leftover fabric from the bottom of garments with the hem attached)**
- **Chalk, pencil, or a fabric crayon**
- **Ruler (or straightedge object)**
- **Ribbon (I used satin ribbon, but any kind will work.)**
- **Scissors**
- **Straight pins**
- **Sewing machine, or hand needle, and thread (sew option)**
- **Safety pins or fabric glue (no-sew option)**
- **Plastic photo sleeves— optional**

I'm a shoe gal, but I never buy retail, so all my shoes from sample sales or Buffalo Exchange are usually sans boxes. I have an over-the-door shoe rack for the knock-around ones, but what to do with the nicer pairs that just chill at the bottom of my closet? Shoe bags! Shoe bags made from excess fabric! That's right, we're going to craft simple shoe bags to fill with heels and flats that can be layered on top of each other without getting damaged.

1. Take excess fabric cut from the bottom of a garment; the bits with the hem attached.

2. Measure 1 foot in width and 1½ feet in length and

trim out your piece. I'm making this to fit a pair of flats, but use whatever amount works best for the size of your shoes, as this can be adjusted.

3. Turn material so the underside is facing out.

4. Fold in half and pin the edges all the way around.

5. Begin to stitch around the rectangle, beginning at the bottom left corner and up to where the hem begins.

6. Trim the edges and turn inside out.

7. A ribbon will soon be weaved through the space in the hem, so pin the edges of the hem opening inside and hand stitch the raw edges down.

8. Attach a safety pin to a matching (color coordinated) ribbon, and weave through the open space in the hem until it comes out the other side.

Add shoes, tie the ribbon in a bow, and store!

TAKE THAT ORGANIZATION FURTHER

If you need to organize by your own little Dewey Decimal System, hand stitch or safety pin a thin sheet of plastic (use old photo albums) to the top of the bag and insert a photo or handwritten description of the shoe to see what you've got inside!

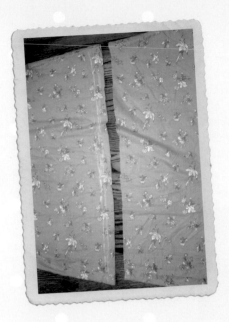

look #2

apron

Dressipe

- **Excess fabric leftovers (I used the leftover fabric from chapter 18: Yellow Dress, p. 185.)**
- **Chalk, pencil, or a fabric crayon**
- **Ruler (or straightedge object)**
- **Scissors**
- **Straight pins**
- **Ribbon (I used grosgrain)**
- **Sewing machine, or hand needle, and thread (sew option)**
- **Fabric glue (no-sew option)**

I have a lovely vintage apron in my possession that I got for a quarter, but it looks like it was worn while working under a car. Using this as a template, a new apron is on the way with the use of fabric that's been trimmed and tossed.

1. Measure the fabric for the skirt first. (I'm using the apron that I have as an exact template, 14 inches across and 12 inches lengthwise.) You want to make sure the skirt of the apron fully covers your thighs because flour doesn't fall gracefully.

2. Using a tape measure, begin at one side of your legs (where your arms hit when they're resting by your side)

and measure across to the other side to get your width. For the length start at your waist and measure down to where you want the apron to end. Use these measurements to draw your outline with a marking utensil.

3. Trim around the markings, leaving at least 1 inch extra for the hem.

4. Next, measure the fabric for the top. If you don't want a top to your apron and just want to make a skirt apron, skip to Step 5 and end at Step 8. I went 6 inches across and 9 inches lengthwise. For this top section of the apron, measure from right above the bust to the waist for the length and across the bust for the width.

5. Trim around the markings and leave at least 1 inch extra for the hem.

6. Pin around the edges of both pieces and stitch them either by hand or machine. Fabric glue can be used to affix edges in lieu of sewing.

7. To make a few pleats, which will make the waist smaller and give the apron more of a trapezoid look, gather a pinch (or 1/4 inch to be technical), fold to the left, and repeat. I did this 4 times, copying my template exactly, but adjust to make more or less pleats, depending on taste and fit.

8. Cut the coordinating ribbon next. I like something a little thicker, anything 1 inch and wider. I went with $1^3/_8$ inch ribbon for the waist and a $^7/_8$-inch ribbon for the neck. I cut 30 inches for the waist and 20 inches for the neck. Pin the skirt to the ribbon and sew them together using a straight stitch by machine, a running stitch by hand, or by using fabric glue.

9. Next add the top of the apron to the ribbon. Center the piece, pin it in place, and sew or glue them together.

10. Take 2 lengths of ribbon, about 8 inches each, and stitch or glue them to the top right and left edges of the apron, to be used to secure the apron around the neck.

Time to get my Julia Child on!

POLLY POCKET

Add a pocket to the skirt, if you'd like, by taking a square bit of fabric with a strip of ribbon at the top, pinning down, and stitching or gluing the three sides in place, leaving the top open to hold measuring spoons or your phone.

chapter sixteen

accessories

Mel: Do you know what time it is?

Cher: A watch doesn't really go with this outfit, Dad.

Even though almost every word Cher from *Clueless* spewed from her mouth was bond, this I disagreed with because I think watches, bracelets, rings, oh my, go with any outfit, and honestly, the more the merrier! When I need a little zhuzhing to primp up a plain ensemble, adding a few bangles or a big faux cocktail ring tends to do the trick.

I've got a treasure trove of goodies I've collected over the years courtesy of eBay, the Rose Bowl flea market, estate sales, and hand-me-downs from my grandma. However, being a crafter, there are some other handmade pieces in my collections **(bracelets made from buttons and cardboard medallion necklace covered in rhinestones)** that garner the same, "hey, that's cute, where did you get it?"

Let's create a few pieces of flair and add some glam to the accessory drawer. With the following tricks, the question of whether "you prefer fashion victim or ensemble-y challenged" will never be brought up. Promise.

appliqués turned headbands & barrettes

Dressipe

- **Not-so-awesome garment with awesome appliqués**
- **Seam ripper**
- **Scissors**

Sometimes dresses or shirts are just meant to be without these extra details—sometimes they'd just look better somewhere else.

1. Use a seam ripper to remove stitches holding down any appliqués to a garment. Sequins are delicate, so be careful when removing!

2. Now that the appliqués are removed, it's time to attach them somewhere else.

DIY HeaDBanD

Dressipe

- **Appliqués from not-so-awesome garment or bedazzled fabric (see page 161)**
- **Glue gun and glue sticks**
- **Felt**
- **Scissors**
- **Headband (I used a Goody band.)**

1. Cut two pieces from the felt that will fit beneath the appliqué and hot glue one to the back of the sequined piece. (I went with circular shapes because they covered most of the back of the floral piece without being seen.)

2. Hot glue the headband to the felted appliqué, then glue the other felt circle on top of it.

Let the hot glue cool for a few seconds and your headband is head ready!

DIY
Barrette

Dressipe

- **Appliqués from not-so-awesome garment or bedazzied fabric (see page 161)**
- **Glue gun and glue sticks**
- **Felt**
- **Scissors**
- **Barrettes or snap clips (I got a multi-pack from Michaels.)**

1. Cut a piece of felt larger than the clip, but smaller than the appliqué.

2. Glue barrette to felt, then glue the appliqué to the felted area.

3. Let the hot glue cool for a few seconds and it's clip time!

Both pieces will give rad appliqués a new and shinier life in the tresses. All I need is Rumplestiltskin to weave me 24K gold locks to match!

look #2

DYED SHOES

Dressipe

- **Dyeable shoes or leftover bridesmaid heels in celery** ☺
- **Fabric dye (I used RIT dye in Cherry Red.)**
- **Salt**
- **Dye pot**
- **Container to dye shoes in (I used a plastic shoebox from Bed Bath & Beyond.)**
- **Plastic or rubber gloves**
- **Work space cover (newspaper or plastic garbage bag)**

Julia Roberts knew just how to make those boots work in *Pretty Woman,* and she also knew how to maintain them—hello, Sharpie! These shoes I found were white satin (probably a wedding cast-off) but had some red crayon marks that didn't scream "buy me," except that's just what I did.

1. Using the dye techniques from chapter 13, boil water on the stove top, add salt, and add the dye color. (Because of the red marks, I went with Cherry Red to match and hide.)

2. Wet the shoes, saturating them totally.

3. If your shoes won't fit in your dye pot, you can use a plastic container large enough to hold them. (I used a plastic shoebox from my closet, which was the perfect fit.) Add the wet shoes to the container filled with the red dye—make sure you cover your work space with newspaper or a plastic garbage bag in case of any spillage.

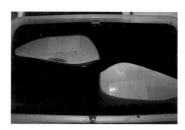

4. Let the shoes saturate long enough for the shade to hide the markings or until the desired color has been reached. I let them soak overnight, removed them from the box with rubber gloves, and washed them with warm water followed by cold to get all the excess dye out. To dry, I hung the slingbacks on a hanger in my shower with a few layers of newspaper underneath to catch drippings.

I had brand-new kicks with no signs of crayon at the end of the makeover! Now, where's my Kit De Luca screaming "Work it baby, work it, do it" while I strut in my new heels?

look #3

RHINESTONE purse

Dressipe

- **Flat-sided purse or clutch**
- **Rhinestone setter and hot-fix stones (I used Darice's duo but you can also use a glue gun or E-6000 glue sticks and toothpicks with flat-backed rhinestones.)**
- **Sharpie Super Fine in contrasting color, if desired, to mark pattern**

I'm a bling girl—I love rhinestones on just about anything. I've had this purse since high school (it's Esprit, circa 1994) and was ready to Goodwill it, but felt that I could add some serious mileage to it with just one thing, rhinestones. I wanted to give it an art deco feel, so I decided on clear stones in a design of vertical stripes, starting on both ends.

1. Use a rhinestone setter and accompanying hot-fix rhinestones (they've got glue on the back that heats up!) to affix. Glue guns and epoxy glue work too—go with whatever is easiest and cleanest to work with. (For smaller stones like these, 5 mm setters work best for me); ulti-

mately, you don't want glue to squeeze out from under the edges when the stones are pushed down.

2. Turn on the setter, heat the stones, and affix them in your chosen pattern or heat the glue gun, dab the backs of the rhinestones with glue, and affix. The stones dry in a matter of seconds.

If you're making a design that doesn't follow edges or you want more of a pattern to follow, mark the spots where the rhinestones would sit with a fine-tipped Sharpie.

For a purse that's pushing twenty years old, not too shabby!

purse flair

Sequins, glitter, or flat buttons are also stellar choices to adorn a purse! Try googly eyes, pom-poms, or feathers for more of a 3-D feel.

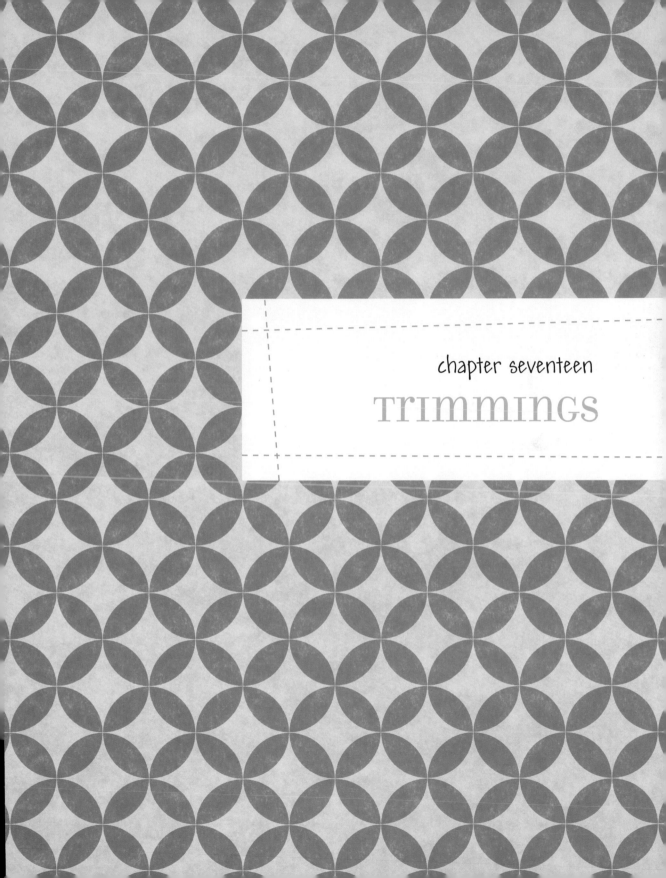

chapter seventeen

TRIMMINGS

I love Thanksgiving and the divine sides that go along with the turkey (taters 'n' gravy), and I can spend hours at the mecca of trim, M&J Trimming in NY, touching, salivating, and gazing over all the lace, sequins, and beaded trim goodness. I think my dream vacation would be camping out inside to hang with the colorful ribbons, fringe, and rickrack. Yeah, some people choose Jamaica as their getaway, and I choose a craft store.

I love how these accents can add just that extra bit of flair to a piece—ribbon can work as a makeshift belt, fringe can be stitched to a dress to make a DIY flapper costume, and lace can be used as straps for a sundress (see chapter 4).

By giving something a little glitz, a little frill, or even a little help if a garment happens to be too short or needs some TLC, it's trim to the rescue for that somethin' somethin' or to hide and cover up those problematic areas.

HIDE PROBLEM areas WITH TrIM

Dressipe

- **Garment with fraying edges**
- **Trim (ribbon, lace, rick-rack, feathers, or fringe—whatever your heart desires!)**
- **Scissors**
- **Straight pins**
- **Sewing machine, or hand needle, and thread (sew option)**
- **Fabric glue (no-sew option)**

The edges of this thrifted bolero were shag central and had started to look like feathers were growing from them. With any piece that has this raw-edged issue, trim will give it a pronto face-lift.

1. Find a shade of ribbon, trim, or lace that matches the piece.

2. Pin the trim to the edges. (For this piece, I pinned the flat center of the ruffled trim to all the exposed edges.)

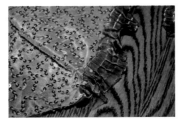

3. Once the trim is pinned down, lace up your sewing machine with matching thread and begin to stitch it in place, or glue it to the edges.

Three easy steps—procure trim, pin in place, and stitch or glue down—to bring something from shaggy to chic. They call me Mr. Boombastic.

look #2

LENGTHEN WITH TRIM

Dressipe

- **Too-short garment**
- **Trim (thicker ribbon, lace, fringe, etc)**
- **Scissors**
- **Straight pins**
- **Sewing machine, or hand needle, and thread (sew option)**
- **Fabric glue (no-sew option)**

This dress was a smidge too short, so I had two options: pass it along to a shorter friend or add trim. I decided to go the trim route! Trim can be a great extension—add a bit of trim to the bottom of a garment and you've got another few inches to work with.

1. Find a shade of trim that matches or complements the piece.

2. Pin the trim to the edges. (For this piece, I pinned the edge of the pink ribbon completely around the bottom of the dress.)

3. Once the trim is pinned down, lace up your sewing machine with matching thread and begin to stitch it in place with a straight stitch, or hand sew with a running stitch all around. For non-sewers, grab some fabric glue, dab the edges, and stick the trim in place.

Now there will be fewer worries that you'll pull a Sharon Stone, *Basic Instinct*–style move, unless you really want to use that ice pick.

look #3

DIY BELTS

Dressipe

- **Trim (beaded trim, ribbon, lace, or leather)**
- **Tape measure**
- **Velcro**
- **Hand needles and thread (if desired)**

I'm a sucker for belts—my favorite in the collection is one that my dad wore in high school, which I borrowed and, well, kept. It's cool, though—he gave me his blessing. **Blessing = forgot about it.**

Belts are super easy to make, and with any sort of fun trim and Velcro, you can have a shape-maker around your waist in no time.

1. Grab your trim. (I found great beaded trim and gold leathery trim for cheap at the fabric store.)

2. Measure your waist with a tape measure and cut the ribbon to size.

3. Peel off adhesive backing and attach Velcro to each end of the trim. The Velcro hooks right side up on the lower piece and loops on the underside of the upper piece.

4. To ensure that the Velcro sticks you can also hand sew a quick running stitch around the edges of both sides, if desired. This should keep it in place after putting it on and taking it off over and over again.

For an extra accent, tie a bow with the trim remnants and stitch down or hot glue to the end of the top ribbon.

Waist cinchers complete!

OTHER NON-TRADISH BELTS

For a really easy belt, use a scarf from your collection; a long, thick chain necklace; or even a man's tie around your waist.

chapter eighteen

BOO-BOO FIXES

I'm a bit of a klutz. I garnered the nickname "Olive Oyl" in college for accidentally using my mascara as lip gloss one night. **(What? It was dark.)** I bump into things often and bruise like the dickens. Band-Aids fix my boo-boos, but what about those problematic issues found on shirts or dresses? Holes, spots, worn out elastic around the waist . . . Band-Aids don't work for everything.

Do dresses with large gaping holes on the seam or disintegrating elastic from hanging in your closet too long sound familiar at all? These holes or bits of funky elastic usually may be reason enough to pass over a top while sifting through boxes of stuff at garage sales or to toss into the giveaway pile when spring cleaning, but wait . . . these pieces can be salvaged! If you're thrifting, you can probably even talk the seller down in price because of the damage! Bargaining skills and being nice are *muy importante!*

Holes and elastic issues like these can easily be mended. It's all about the Cinderella treatment for these garments to take them from torn to magnificent, just like those mice who made Cinderelly's dress ball-worthy, except we've got height on those crafty rodents.

rip on seam

Dressipe

- **Garment with ripped seam**
- **Straight pins**
- **Sewing machine, or hand needle, and thread (sew option)**
- **Safety pins (no-sew option)**

Tears that happen right on a seam are easily fixed with a quick hand stitch or run under the machine. Just because a navel is popping through or there's a little breeze at the waist doesn't mean it has to get tossed curbside!

1. Pin the sections of the seam that have come undone.

2. Grab a matching spool and thread your machine or thread the needle if you're sans a sewing machine. Safety pins also do the trick in closing up the hole as a no-sew option.

3. Stitch over the holes by hand or by machine and go back and forth a few times to close up shop.

From donate pile to a day at the park.

boo-boo fixes ⊗ 185

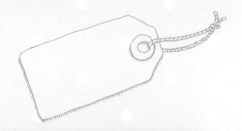

FLea market tricks

- Head to the party late! You may not get the pick of the litter arriving later on in the day, but you will get those sellers wanting to make fast deals so they don't have to repack unsold merch.

- All the single(s) ladies! Bring one-dollar bills! It's much easier to barter when you have $1s instead of $10s or $20s—nobody likes being talked down from $10 to $7 and then given a $10 as payment.

- BYOB! Not the BYOB that you're thinking of. Bring Your Own Bag while you're shopping! Many vendors don't have bags to give you your loot in, so instead of trying to carry everything in your hands, bring a canvas tote or beach bag to house your goodies. This ensures nothing slips through your fingers and gives you more freedom to touch and pick through vintage gold!

- Wear fitted pants, a fitted top, and shoes that are easy to take off and put on. When you're booth hoppin' without fitting rooms, wearing leggings or opaque tights and a camisole underneath a cardigan or summer dress is ideal for changing in front of everyone. It'll just look like you're in yoga gear in the middle of the rows. Same with shoes—slip-ons or flip-flops in the warm weather are most ideal!

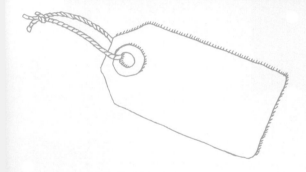

look #2

magenta Dress— Stretched Out waist

Dressipe

- **Too-big dress**
- **Vintage pin**

There are some dresses in my closet that I love but have gotten stretched out over the years. This is the easiest trick in the book and it only involves two things: the dress and a vintage pin.

1. Put on the dress and gather the area at the waist that is too baggy or stretched out.

2. Stick the vintage pin through the dress, gathering the excess material, and clasp it.

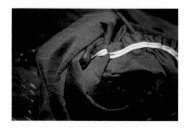

And you're dunzo, with a dress that fits like a glove once again!

PIN-UP GIRL

For pieces with spots on them that just pain you to get rid of . . . hold up, wait a minute! Make a collage of pins or patches to cover it up. Art on your chest to hide a spot of spilled Bolognese can be a totally covert operation with excellent results!

chapter nineteen
1 dress, 7 ways

always wanted to rock the Catholic school uniform on a day-to-day basis because I loved the plaid skirts, the blazers, the ties, and the argyle socks **(unforch, I ended up going the public school route)**. The idea of wearing the same thing every day isn't the reason why I liked the uniform (obviously)—I liked the idea of pairing the ten or so options in different ways so that it would feel like I was wearing something new each day. Navy blazer, yellow blouse, and plaid tie one day, and white blouse, yellow vest, and navy skirt another day . . . the options are really endless, especially when you can work some accessories and argyle sock colors in.

I love the idea of amazing staple pieces that can have lots of versatile looks with the addition of jewelry, tights, layering pieces, shoes, etc. You don't need to have a closet that's overflowing with garments à la Carrie Bradshaw **(anyone else question how she was able to fit all those designer duds in her Manhattan closet, pre-Big?)** to have a week/month/year full of different looks. It's all about using what you've got and working them in different ways.

For this chapter, you're getting seven different looks for the price of one. And the price of this one was thrifted for a mere $5. Yeah, for five buckaroos, a week's worth of ensembles will be laid out. From the workday to girls' night out, and brunch to cocktails, this one piece will work for them all with the addition of things you already have in your own closet!

LBD
reDO

Dressipe

- **Black dress, if going the LBD route**
- **Chalk, pencil, or a fabric crayon**
- **Ruler (or straightedge object)**
- **Scissors**
- **Straight pins**
- **Thread**
- **Sewing machine, or hand needle, and thread (sew option)**
- **Stitch Witchery (no-sew option)**
- **Assorted wardrobe items to add**

A perfect-fitting little black dress is a necessity. No wonder Audrey Hepburn has remained a fashion icon for so long . . . it never goes out of style.

This piece had an excellent neckline and fit like a glove, but there were some issues (satin cuffs and longer length with a too-long slit) that I wanted to fix to make it a timeless piece that will work over and over again. Don't let the satin cuffs deter you when making a purchase decision. WWMD? (What Would Marisa Do?) If the dress fits, you must buy it!

1. After marking the length, trim any unwanted areas from the dress. (I trimmed the sleeves up to my elbow and shortened the bottom hem.)

2. Pin the raw edges under and stitch new seams either by hand or machine. Use Stitch Witchery for a completely no-sew route. (See pp. 117–118 for Stitch Witchery instructions)

Dress is done and it's time to get dressed for the week!

look #1

Pair with some pearls and black heels and you're ready to go. This can moonlight as a Halloween costume too. If you're feeling the *Breakfast at Tiffany*'s vibe, add some black gloves and a cigarette holder to channel Holly Golightly.

look #2

Put on vintage blouse that ties at the neck underneath the dress, and you're finished! Slightly *Mad Men,* the perfect dress for cocktail hour.

look #3

Add a motorcycle jacket, boots, and a statement necklace to give the dress a bit more edge to rock out at a concert.

look #4

For a day at the office, a cardigan, fun belt, and some ballet flats do the trick. You'd totally be Scranton BFF's with Kelly Kapoor, talking about Beyoncé, sno-cones, and pink in that ensemble.

look #5

Toss on a bold, billowy caftan, top, or tunic, and you're golden. Whether it's covered in sequins, stripes, or an electric shade of blue, it'll add a bit of pow for a fun night out with the gals.

look #6

Take an elastic-waisted skirt and add it on top for another DIY dress in just seconds. The fitted top of the dress paired with the pouffy bottom softens the sleekness and adds a bit more femininity, just right for a date night with a cutie-pie.

look #7

Opaque tights, an open-front blouse, loafers, and a tote bag gives this dress a casual makeover just right for toting the laptop to the coffee shop or meeting up for Sunday brunch.

where to shop

craft, supply, and fabric stores

Michaels—michaels.com

Jo-Ann—joann.com

Staples—staples.com

M&J Trimming—mjtrim.com

Blick Art Materials—dickblick.com

Pearl Paint—pearlpaint.com

Home Depot—homedepot.com

Mood Fabrics—moodfabrics.com

Dollar Tree and other 99-cent stores—dollartree.com

thrift-store chains

Goodwill—goodwill.org

Salvation Army—salvationarmy.com

Value Village—valuevillage.com

Savers—savers.com

Thrift Town Thrift Store—thrifttown.com

smaller vintage and thrift store fan faves

Alabama—Unclaimed Baggage Center, Scottsboro

Alaska—Turn A Leaf Thrift Stores, Wasilla

Arizona—Save the Family Thrift Store, Mesa

Arkansas—Wolfe Street Thrift Store, Little Rock

California—Heavenly Treasures Thrift & Gift, Santa Rosa

Colorado—Arc Thrift Store, Colorado Springs

Connecticut—Helping Hands Community Thrift Store & Furniture Bank, New Haven

Delaware—Encore Thrift Shop, Lewes

D.C.—Annie Creamcheese, Georgetown

Florida—Junior League Thrift Shop, Gainesville

Georgia—Frock of Ages, Atlanta

Hawaii—Assistance League of Hawaii, Honolulu

Idaho—Idaho Youth Ranch, Boise

Illinois—Village Discount Outlet, Chicago

Indiana—The Bloomington Thrift Shop Inc., Bloomington

Iowa—Atomic Garage, West Des Moines

Kansas—T-La-Re, Manhattan

Kentucky—Clothes Lion, Bowling Green

Louisiana—Miss Claudia's Vintage Clothing & Costumes, New Orleans

Maine—Another Chance Animal Rescue Thrift Shop, North Berwick

Maryland—Montgomery County Thrift Shop, Bethesda

Massachusetts—Urban Renewals, Allston; Chicken Alley Thrift Shop, Vineyard Haven

Michigan—Value World, 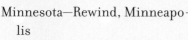 Detroit

Minnesota—Rewind, Minneapolis

Mississippi—L & L Odds & Ends Resale, Ridgeland

Missouri—DAV Thrift Stores, Kansas City

Montana—Sacks Thrift Store, Bozeman

 Nebraska—Blue Flamingo, Omaha

Nevada—The Gypsy Den, Las Vegas

New Hampshire—Upscale Resale, Portsmouth

New Jersey—Ye Olde Thrift Shoppe, Red Bank

New Mexico—Now & Again, Taos

New York—Volunteers of America, Elmira

North Carolina—Assistance League of Charlotte Thrift Shop, Charlotte

North Dakota—The Arc of Bismarck, Bismarck

Ohio—Ohio Thrift, locations across Ohio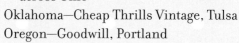

Oklahoma—Cheap Thrills Vintage, Tulsa

Oregon—Goodwill, Portland

Pennsylvania—The Care and Share Shoppes, Souderton; Jubilee Store, Lebanon

Rhode Island—Foreign Affair Warehouse, Providence

South Carolina—SC Thrift & Resale Store, McClellanville

South Dakota—Closet to Closet, Aberdeen

Tennessee—Legacy Vintage Clothing, Knoxville

Texas—Lula B's Antique Mall, Dallas

Utah—Decades Vintage Clothing, Salt Lake City

Vermont—Listen Thrift Store, White River Junction

 Virginia—Diversity Thrift, Richmond

Washington—St. Vincent De Paul Society, Monroe

West Virginia—Retrodini, Berkeley Springs

Wisconsin—The Bargain Garden Thrift Shop, Appleton

Wyoming—Donna's Wear It Again Apparel, Cheyenne

Canada—The Cat's Meow Thrift Shop, Ontario

UK—Mind Shop, Oxford

TROUBLESHOOTING

· **What if you open too much of a seam with a seam ripper?**

Fear not! Re-stitch what you opened up by hand or machine or use a safety pin to secure closed. Check out chapter 18: Yellow Dress, p. 185, to see complete steps.

· **What if you accidentally cut a hole in the fabric?**

Whoopsie! Either try to mend it from the inside, hand stitching the hole closed or perhaps toss a vintage pin, appliqué, or patch on top of the spot. If it's toward the bottom of the piece, cut it shorter and make it a tunic.

· **What if you leave a garment in dye for too long and it gets darker than you wanted?**

1. You can try using a color remover, like RIT Color Remover, to adjust and make it lighter.

2. Roll with the dark color flow!

· **What if you have an unruly zipper on your jeans that won't stay up?**

Easy peasy. Take a rubber band and insert it into the square hole at the top of the zipper itself. Pull it halfway through so it looks like a figure 8. Take one end of the band and put it through the other end and pull. There will be one big loop now when you zip your zipper; wrap it around the button a few times, then put the button through the buttonhole on the jeans.

· **How to get dye out of countertops?**

If you went a little dye crazy and some color got on your tabletops, here are a few potential fixes that may help remove. (These are not guaranteed . . .)

1. Baking soda and water—mix these two together until you get a paste and use an old toothbrush to make circles on the counter.

2. Vinegar—try using a sponge and this miracle worker. (Apple cider vinegar is awesome for burns too, per an old wives' tale. If you happen to burn a finger baking or using a glue gun, immediately pour vinegar on top of the burn to make it heal faster.)

3. Magic Eraser. These puppies are brilliant, from marks on walls to dirty laptop keys to getting color off of the counter.

· **How do you remove deodorant marks from clothing?**

Those pesky white lines will be gone in a matter of seconds by using a like fabric and rubbing it against the mark. I'll grab the bottom of a dress and make little circles over a deod mark at my waist to remove. Fast fix!

- **I used chalk to make lines on my dress and there is still some there. How do I remove?**

    Use the same trick as above with the deodorant. Take a like fabric, make circular motions on top, and the lines will be gone.

- **Help, I got Fray Check on my jeans!**

    No worries—take some rubbing alcohol and a cotton ball and pretend like you're taking off nail polish with nail polish remover.

- **The drawstring came out of my pj's, do I have to toss?**

    No need to toss—use the trick from chapter 4: Sundresses (see p. 37). Take a safety pin and pin the edge of the string that came out. Use the pin as your guide and push it all the way around the seam until it comes out the other end. Pants are like brand-new.

acknowledgments

To the amazing, lovely, creative (the list could go on…) readers who have been following and supporting New Dress a Day since day 1 ($364 to go) until now. I love and appreciate each of you and am forever grateful for your presence. You're my blogosphere family and I am one lucky gal.

To Mom, Dad, and Dane, my (Plymouth) rocks who have given me all the love, support, help, advice, shooting locations, and heart I could ever wish for. I'm lucky to have spent my years under the same roof as you. xo

To the rest of my family and friends—what an amazing unit to be a part of. The endless support is overwhelming and so greatly appreciated. Love you.

To Jeremy Tarr, Jordan Whitley, and Max Roman, the creative geniuses who made the photos stunning and the words make sense. You're already hired for the next book ☺.

Agent extraordinaire Meg Thompson for being my dream partner and simply being awesome.

To everyone at Ballantine for believing in me—my editor, Porscha Burke; publisher, Jane von Mehren; the lovely designer, Liz Cosgrove; my production team: Shona McCarthy, Sarah Feightner, and Jenn Backe; and publicity mavens Ella Maslin, Sharon Propson, and Susan Corcoran. I wore the pages out of my *The Random House Book of Poetry for Children* when I was a kid and now Random House is publishing my book. It's a total dream.

I'm forever indebted to all the friend-tographers who helped document my daily outfit journeys while hanging out and those who actually posed in the pics! (This is like my HS yearbook page; get ready for the initials!) Without their support and keen skill for snapping pictures, I would have been the only one to see my daily outfits. First round of drinks is on me guys. You rule. AB, AB, AK, AM, AR, AW, BL, BSM, CB, CJ, DG, DL, DL, DL, DM, DR, EW, EL, JB, JG, JMT, JS, JS, JS, JS, JT, JW, KL, KN, LB, LG, LJ, LP, LS, MA, MK, ML, MM, MP, MR, MR, MRC, MW, MW, NC, NK, PB, PF, PR, REF, RM, RN, RO, SJ, SPR, SR, SZ, TC, TJ, TT.

CREDITS

Photographer—Jordan Whitley
Creative director—Jeremy Tarr
Hair and makeup:
- Carly Ryan, before shots (facebook.com/BombshellBeautyEnt)
- Natasha Marcelina, after shots (natashamarcelina.com)

Location—The Farmer's Daughter Hotel (farmersdaughterhotel.com)
Shoes provided by Seychelles (seychelles.com)
Additional clothing provided by Alternative Apparel (alternativeapparel.com), LOFT (loft.com), and The Hellers (wearethehellers.com).
Additional accessories provided by Lulu Frost (lulufrost.com), Oakley (Oakley.com), Chilli Beans (chillibeans.com), and Frieda & Nellie (friedaandnellie.com).
Thanks to Tulip/Aleene's (ilovetocreate.com), Simplicity (simplicity.com), RIT Dye (ritdye.com), Darice (darice.com), and Rowenta (rowenta.com) for additional support!

notepad

I hope you enjoy this book, but more important I hope that it has inspired some of your creativity! Here's space to create your own personal inspiration boards. Add notes, checklists, measurements, cutouts from your favorite fashion magazines, color ideas, or even doodles of your own designs. It's like Pinterest, but on actual paper!

measurements/fabric amounts/ribbon lengths

_____
_____
_____
_____
_____
_____
_____
_____
_____
_____
_____

flea market/thrift store/garage sale/my closet checklist . . .
project pieces i'm looking for . . .

- ☐ _____
- ☐ _____
- ☐ _____
- ☐ _____
- ☐ _____
- ☐ _____
- ☐ _____
- ☐ _____
- ☐ _____
- ☐ _____

- ☐ _____
- ☐ _____
- ☐ _____
- ☐ _____
- ☐ _____
- ☐ _____
- ☐ _____
- ☐ _____
- ☐ _____
- ☐ _____

supplies i have	supplies i need
_____	_____
_____	_____
_____	_____
_____	_____
_____	_____
_____	_____
_____	_____
_____	_____
_____	_____
_____	_____
_____	_____

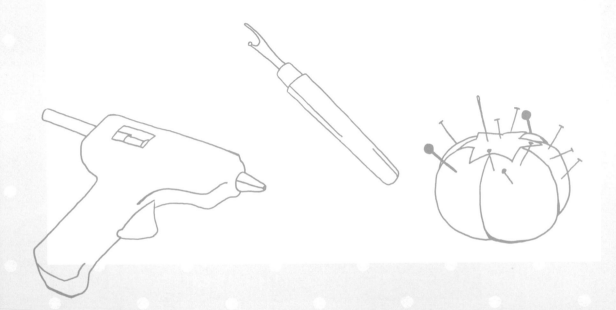

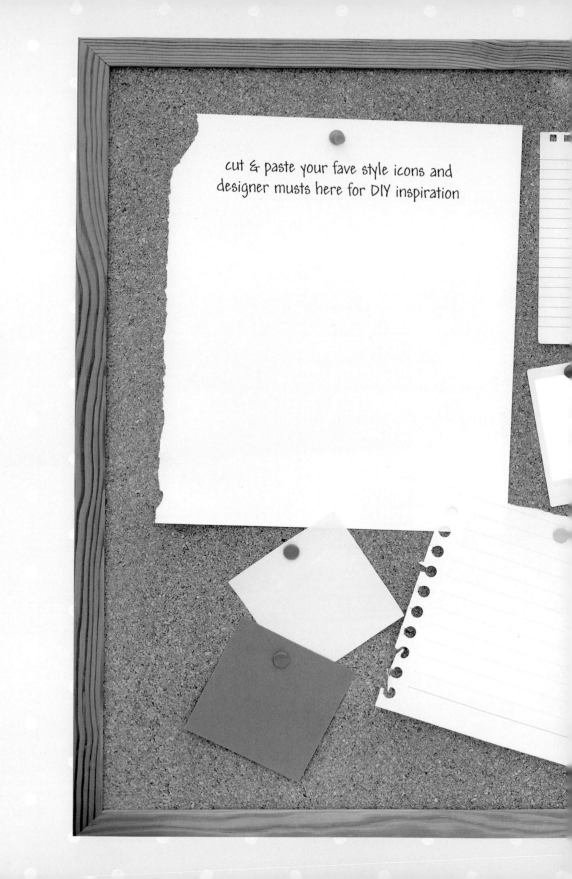

cut & paste your fave style icons and
designer musts here for DIY inspiration

my project ideas

index

About the Author

MARISA LYNCH is a fashion blogger, consultant, and founder of the blog New Dress a Day. A graduate of the University of Southern California, she is a frequent guest on E! Entertainment Television and has appeared on *The Early Show* and been featured in the *Los Angeles Times*, *Time*, and *Bust*, among other publications. You can usually find her sifting through vintage jewelry at the flea market, scrolling through Twitter while waiting on line at Starbucks (say hi @newdressaday), behind a sewing machine with Justin Timberlake pumping from the speakers, or falling asleep on top of her laptop while blogging into the wee hours with *Late Night with Jimmy Fallon* keeping her company. She lives in Los Angeles.